THE
OFFICIAL
COOKBOOK

THE
OFFICIAL
COOKBOOK

TOTALLY DELICIOUS RECIPES
INSPIRED BY THE FILM

KIM LAIDLAW
ILLUSTRATED BY **LISA MALTBY**

RUNNING PRESS
PHILADELPHIA

Running Press
Hachette Book Group
1290 Avenue of the Americas, New York, NY 10104
www.runningpress.com
@Running_Press

First Edition: April 2024

Published by Running Press, an imprint of Hachette Book Group, Inc. The Running Press name and logo are trademarks of Hachette Book Group, Inc.

The Hachette Speakers Bureau provides a wide range of authors for speaking events. To find out more, go to www.hachettespeakersbureau.com or email HachetteSpeakers@hbgusa.com.

Running Press books may be purchased in bulk for business, educational, or promotional use. For more information, please contact your local bookseller or the Hachette Book Group Special Markets Department at Special.Markets@hbgusa.com.

The publisher is not responsible for websites (or their content) that are not owned by the publisher.

Print book cover and interior design by Jenna McBride.
Food illustrations by Lisa Maltby.
Food icons and patterns are from Getty Images.

Library of Congress Cataloging-in-Publication Data
Names: Laidlaw, Kim, author. | Maltby, Lisa, illustrator.
Title: Clueless the official cookbook : totally delicious recipes inspired by the film / Kim Laidlaw ; illustrated by Lisa Maltby.
Other titles: Clueless (Motion picture)
Description: First edition. | Philadelphia : Running Press, [2024] | Includes index. | Summary: "Clueless: The Official Cookbook brings all the '90s nostalgia from the cult classic film straight to your kitchen with 50 totally delectable dishes, drinks, apps, sides, and more, inspired by one of the most unforgettable and beloved comedies of all time"—Provided by publisher.
Identifiers: LCCN 2023016184 (print) | LCCN 2023016185 (ebook) | ISBN 9780762483686 (hardcover) | ISBN 9780762483891 (ebook)
subjects: LCSH: Cooking, American. | LCGFT: Literary cookbooks
Classification: LCC TX715 .L185 2024 (print) | LCC TX715 (ebook) | DDC 641.5973—dc23/eng/20230417
LC record available at https://lccn.loc.gov/2023016184
LC ebook record available at https://lccn.loc.gov/2023016185

ISBNs: 978-0-7624-8368-6 (hardcover), 978-0-7624-8389-1 (ebook)

Printed in China

APS

10 9 8 7 6 5 4 3 2 1

Contents

Introduction

Witty, charming, privileged Cher Horowitz
leads the pack at her Beverly Hills high school
in Amy Heckerling's 1990s cult classic *Clueless.*
The film—a cleverly reshaped version of *Emma*
by Jane Austen—follows the buoyantly funny,
motherless 15-year-old hero, Cher, as she navigates
teenagehood. Through the eyes of style-obsessed Cher,
we join in the fun of makeovers, the roller-coaster ride of
crushes and friendships, and the social hierarchy of high school.

Inspired by the snacks, munchies, and meals highlighted throughout the
film, the Southern California healthy-eating craze, and the best of the 1990s,
the recipes in this cookbook celebrate the adventures and calamities of Cher,
her friends, and her family. Take-it-with-you options in the "Breakfast on the
Go" chapter, like the Jump-in-the-Car Breakfast Bars (page 6) and Gnarly
Skateboarder's Breakfast Sandos (page 12), remind us of the chaos of getting
to school on time.

Homemade versions of the snack foods that litter high school cafeteria
lunch tables are found in Better-Than-Bagged Potato Chips (page 29), Off-the-
Diet Popcorn (page 24), and Dirty Diet Coke Mocktails (page 152). And school
cafeteria fare is represented in recipes like Not-Your-Cafeteria Spicy Baked
Potato Wedges (page 35) and Teachers' Lounge Italian Tuna Pasta Salad (page
64). Coffee Lover's Coffee Cake (page 8), Desirable Chocolate Truffles (page
128), and Don't Burn the Chocolate Chip Cookies (page 130) showcase teens
and teachers navigating the ins and outs of crushes and love. And Party in the
Valley Pretzel Bites (page 20) and Root Beer "Pool Party" Floats (page 148)
recall raucous high school parties.

Family time, in the form of awkward dinners and late-night legal cases, sparks meals like Chuckleheads Asparagus Quiche (page 84) with Mixed Greens Salad Forever! (page 57) and Midnight Snack Burgers (page 88). Throughout, Cher chides her dad to stay healthy by eating low-fat foods and drinking juice, a trend of the '90s. Dad's Healthy Tropical "Vitamin C" Orange Smoothies (page 144) and Cut-Your-Cholesterol Salmon and Spring Vegetable Fettuccine (page 92) fit the bill, and California Healthy Veggie Burgers (page 99) and So-Lo-Cal Chopped Chicken, Avocado, and Herb Salad (page 66) are truly SoCal health–inspired.

Beauty makeovers, arguments (and harmony) with friends, and the ins and outs of being popular in high school influenced recipes for Makeover Turkey Sandwiches (page 54), So-Cheesy Roasted Garlic Breadsticks (page 27), and Festival Sausage Sandwiches (page 60). And, of course, as fashion is one of the focal points of the film, the Cute Plaid Lemon Sugar Cookies (page 132) honor Cher's emblematic yellow-and-blue plaid outfit.

The recipes in this cookbook bring the personalities and narrative of *Clueless* to life—you'll find quick breakfasts, teen-approved snacks, family meals worth fighting over, late-night snacks, and lunches that put anything served at the school cafeteria to shame. It's a celebration of a particular time and place and a tribute to this enduring, charming comedy. So dive in, eat up, and enjoy!

CHAPTER ONE
Breakfast on the Go

Morning is hectic in the Horowitz household: Cher must choose the perfect outfit and make sure her father, Mel—a very important litigator ("the scariest kind of lawyer")—gets some healthy vitamin C. It doesn't leave much time for breakfast, usually grabbed on the way out the door as Cher races to jump in her car and get to school on time. From plump California citrus muffins (page 2) and healthy energy bars (page 6) to pop-in-your-mouth mini pizza bagels (page 14) and Travis's favorite egg sandwich (page 12)—for which he is often tardy, but it's worth it—you'll fall "butt crazy in love" with this chapter. There's even a lavish yogurt, granola, and fruit parfait (page 4) for mornings when you feel Beverly Hills fancy.

MUFFINS

2 cups all-purpose flour

2 teaspoons baking powder

½ teaspoon baking soda

½ teaspoon fine sea salt

2 large eggs

1 cup plain whole-milk yogurt

⅓ cup avocado oil or other neutral oil

⅓ cup granulated sugar

Finely grated zest of 1 orange

Finely grated zest of 1 lemon

1½ cups fresh blueberries (about 9 ounces)

LEMON GLAZE (OPTIONAL)

½ cup confectioners' sugar

1 tablespoon freshly squeezed lemon juice

Sunny CA Citrus Blueberry Muffins

Just-picked Southern California citrus imbue these muffins with enough va-va-voom to give you a fresh start in the morning. And if you're lucky enough to have a citrus tree in your yard, like Cher and her dad, you can simply reach out the window and pluck a lemon off the tree whenever you fancy one. These are also excellent accompaniments to tea in the afternoon when you are trying to get your dad to sign your report card.

Position a rack in the middle of the oven and preheat to 400°F. Spray 16 to 18 cups of two standard muffin pans with cooking spray or line with paper liners.

To make the muffins: In a medium bowl, sift together the flour, baking powder, baking soda, and salt. In a large bowl, whisk together the eggs, yogurt, oil, granulated sugar, and orange and lemon zests until well combined. Add the dry ingredients and blueberries, and stir just until evenly moistened. The batter will be thick.

Scoop the batter into the prepared muffin cups, filling each one about three-quarters full. Bake until the muffins are golden brown and a toothpick inserted into the center comes out clean, about 15 to 17 minutes. Let the muffins cool in the pan on a wire rack for 5 minutes, then unmold onto the rack. Let cool completely.

To make the glaze: If you like, sift the confectioners' sugar into a small bowl. Add the lemon juice and whisk until smooth. Drizzle over the tops of the muffins. Let set for about 15 minutes, then serve.

Beverly Hills Yogurt Parfaits

1⅓ cups (loosely packed) pitted and diced fresh nectarines or peaches (about 2 medium)

1⅓ cups (loosely packed) fresh mixed berries, such as raspberries, blueberries, blackberries, or sliced strawberries

¼ cup fresh orange juice

2 cups vanilla yogurt, plus ½ cup for garnish

2 scant cups of your favorite granola

½ cup (loosely packed) flaked, unsweetened coconut, toasted, for garnish (see Note)

¼ cup chopped roasted almonds, for garnish (see Note)

4 fig bars (optional)

Light yogurt, diet soda, fat-free cookies, or roasted California almonds are usually the lunch of choice for Cher and Dionne. Layering fresh seasonal fruit with yogurt, crunchy granola, and chopped toasted almonds transforms a simple carton of yogurt into an upscale parfait worthy of breakfast in Beverly Hills. If you're using peaches, peel them first. Larger berries should be halved or quartered.

Select 4 of your prettiest serving glasses, each with a 1½- to 2-cup capacity, preferably ones perched on a pedestal.

In a bowl, toss the fruit with the orange juice.

For each parfait, layer ⅓ cup fruit, ¼ cup yogurt, and ¼ cup granola. Repeat the layers for each parfait.

Top each serving with a dollop of yogurt, then garnish with the coconut and almonds, dividing evenly. Bling up your parfait with a totally cute fig bar, if you like!

Note: To toast coconut or nuts, preheat the oven to 350°F. Spread the coconut or nuts on a small baking sheet. Toast, stirring once or twice if needed, until fragrant and golden, about 3 minutes for coconut and 5 to 10 minutes for nuts (depending on the type of nut).

Jump-in-the-Car Breakfast Bars

2 cups old-fashioned rolled oats

1 cup crispy brown rice cereal

⅓ cup chopped dried cherries, dried cranberries, or raisins

⅓ cup chopped roasted peanuts, toasted almonds, or pistachios

⅓ cup mini chocolate chips

½ teaspoon ground cinnamon

½ teaspoon fine sea salt

½ cup packed chopped pitted dates (about 6 ounces)

¼ cup honey

3 tablespoons peanut butter or almond butter

3 tablespoons coconut oil or avocado oil

One of Cher's favorite breakfasts is toasted rice flake cereal as she races out the door to jump in her "loqued out" white SUV that Daddy got her (including four-wheel drive, dual side airbags, and a "monster sound system"). "I don't have a license yet, but I need something to learn on!" she explains. These healthy cereal bars are perfect for anyone "on the go," like Cher!

Preheat the oven to 350°F. Spray a 9-inch-square baking pan lightly with cooking spray, then line the bottom and two sides with parchment paper so the parchment comes up and over two sides of the pan. Set aside.

In a large bowl, combine the oats, rice cereal, dried cherries, peanuts, chocolate chips, cinnamon, and salt. Combine the dates, honey, peanut butter, and oil in a food processor and process to a smooth puree, about 2 minutes. Add the date mixture to the oat mixture and stir until well combined—it helps if you use your hands because the mixture is thick.

Press the granola mixture into the bottom of the pan; use a flat-bottomed glass to press it down into an even layer. Bake until golden brown, about 25 minutes. Cool in the pan on a wire rack until cool enough to handle but still warm, about 15 minutes.

Using the parchment, remove the granola from the pan and place it on a cutting board. Remove the parchment. Cut in half crosswise, then cut into 12 bars total. Let the bars cool completely, then wrap individually with pieces of waxed paper for breakfast on the go.

JOSH:
Hey, James Bond.
In America, we drive on the right
side of the road.

CHER:
I am. You try driving
in platforms.

JOSH:
Look, I gotta get back to school.
Uh, wanna practice parking?

CHER:
What's the point?
Everywhere you go has valet.

BROWN BUTTER STREUSEL

1½ cups all-purpose flour

¾ cup granulated sugar

1 tablespoon instant espresso powder

1 teaspoon ground cinnamon

¼ teaspoon fine sea salt

½ cup unsalted butter

1 teaspoon pure vanilla extract

ESPRESSO CINNAMON SUGAR

1 cup firmly packed light brown sugar

1 tablespoon ground cinnamon

1 tablespoon instant espresso powder

SOUR CREAM CAKE

3 cups all-purpose flour

2½ teaspoons baking powder

½ teaspoon baking soda

1 teaspoon ground cinnamon

1 teaspoon fine sea salt

1 cup sour cream

½ cup whole milk

2 teaspoons pure vanilla extract

1 cup unsalted butter, at room temperature

1¼ cups granulated sugar

3 large eggs

Coffee Lover's Coffee Cake

After receiving poor grades, and in a ploy to loosen their grading standards, Cher and Dionne play matchmakers for two hard-grading teachers at their school—Mr. Hall and Miss Geist—by connecting the teachers through their mutual love of coffee. Later, Cher and Dionne see Mr. Hall and Miss Geist on a school bench sharing the coffee: "Ohhhh, old people can be so sweet!" You'll fall in love with this A+ spiced "coffee" cake, regardless of your age.

Preheat the oven to 350°F. Grease a 13-by-9-inch baking dish with cooking spray, then line the bottom and sides with parchment so the parchment comes up and over the long sides of the dish by about 1 inch.

To make the streusel: In a bowl, whisk together the flour, sugar, espresso powder, cinnamon, and salt. In a small skillet over medium-low heat, melt the butter. Cook, stirring, until the butter becomes fragrant and the milk solids turn nutty brown, about 3 to 4 minutes. Remove from the heat, add the vanilla, and drizzle over the flour mixture. Using a fork and your hands, stir to combine so the mixture is evenly moistened and slightly lumpy in texture. Set aside.

To make the espresso cinnamon sugar: In a bowl, stir together the brown sugar, cinnamon, and espresso powder. Set aside.

To make the cake: In a bowl, whisk together the flour, baking powder, baking soda, cinnamon, and salt. In another bowl, whisk together the sour cream, milk, and vanilla.

Continues on page 10.

In a third bowl, using an electric mixer, beat together the butter and sugar on medium-high speed until fluffy, about 2 minutes. Beat in the eggs one at a time, then scrape down the sides of the bowl with a rubber spatula. Reduce the speed to low and add the flour mixture in 3 additions, alternating with the sour cream mixture in 2 additions. Beat just until the mixture comes together, then scrape down the sides of the bowl and stir to make sure the batter is combined; the batter will be thick.

Using a rubber spatula, spread half the batter into the prepared pan in an even layer. Top with the espresso cinnamon sugar. Dollop the remaining batter on top, spreading into an even layer (it helps to use a small metal spatula or the back of a metal spoon and your fingers to do this). Sprinkle the streusel evenly over the batter.

Bake until golden and set, and a toothpick inserted into the center comes out clean, about 1 hour. Transfer the pan to a wire rack and let the cake cool in the pan for at least 15 minutes. The coffee cake can be made up to 1 day in advance, cooled, covered, and stored at room temperature before serving.

To serve, loosen the short edges with a knife, then lift out the coffee cake using the parchment paper and transfer to a cutting board. Cut into 12 equal squares and serve.

Note: If you prefer your coffee cake more round than rectangle, feel free to sub the 13-by-9-inch pan with two 9-inch round cake pans. Just make sure to split the batter, cinnamon sugar, and streusel evenly across the pans, and start checking for doneness after 30 minutes.

Gnarly Skateboarder's Breakfast Sandos

4 slices Canadian bacon, 8 slices bacon, or 4 pork or vegetarian sausage patties

4 English muffins, split

Salted butter, for spreading and cooking

4 slices American, Cheddar, or another melting cheese

4 large eggs

Fine sea salt and freshly ground black pepper

Travis Birkenstock, with 38 tardies—"by far the most tardies in the [debate] class"—gets up in front of the class to thank everyone in a speech worthy of an award acceptance. His hilarious tribute to the "many, many people who contributed to [his] tardiness" included a nod to his parents for never giving him a lift, and to all the breakfast sandwiches that he lingered over every school morning. These English muffin egg sandwiches are quick to make and will get you on your way to school, work, or wherever you might be headed, hopefully on time.

In a skillet over medium heat, cook the Canadian bacon, bacon, or sausage, turning once, until crisped and cooked through. The timing will depend on what you are cooking, so chill out.

Preheat the broiler, dude. Place the muffin halves, cut side up, on a baking sheet. Broil until lightly toasted. Butter the muffins and slide a mellow slice of cheese on each of the 4 muffin bottoms. Set aside.

Wipe out the skillet and place over medium-low heat. Add a bit of butter to the pan and swirl to coat. Crack the eggs into the skillet and season with salt and pepper. After about 1 minute, break the yolks, and flip the eggs. Cook until done to your liking, 1 to 2 minutes longer for well done.

Place an egg on top of each cheese-topped muffin bottom, then top each with a slice of Canadian bacon (or 2 slices bacon, or a sausage patty). Pop the tops of the muffins on and eat one right away before you're late for school.

Pizza-for-Breakfast Bagel Bites

PIZZA SAUCE

½ cup canned crushed tomatoes

2 teaspoons extra-virgin olive oil

½ teaspoon balsamic vinegar

¼ teaspoon Italian herb seasoning

Fine sea salt and freshly ground black pepper

BAGEL BITES

4 mini bagels, split

4 ounces (about ½ cup) shredded mozzarella cheese

1 teaspoon Italian seasoning

½ cup of your favorite pizza toppings, such as diced pepperoni, sliced black olives, and/or cooked sliced mushrooms (optional)

Chopped fresh basil or flat-leaf parsley, for garnish (optional)

Nothing says "teenager" like cold pizza for breakfast, but you don't have to make a special trip to the mall. Make your own pizza sauce (it's easy and doesn't even require turning on the stove!), or use your favorite store-bought version. You'll find your inner teen eating these bagel bites for breakfast, a midafternoon snack, or any time of day.

To make the pizza sauce: In a bowl, stir together the tomatoes, olive oil, balsamic vinegar, and Italian seasoning. Season with salt and pepper.

To make the bagel bites: Position an oven rack in the upper third of the oven and preheat to 425°F. Lay the bagel halves, cut side up, in an even layer on a baking sheet. Spread 1 tablespoon of the sauce evenly over each bagel half. Divide the cheese between the bagel halves. Sprinkle each with a little Italian seasoning, then sprinkle evenly with the toppings, if using.

Bake until the cheese is melted and the edges of the bagels are toasted and browned, about 10 to 12 minutes. Sprinkle with the fresh herbs if you want them to be extra cute.

CHAPTER TWO
Munchies and More

High school teens fuel up on snacks, and lunch may very well consist of a hodgepodge of eats: bags of chips, some low-fat store-bought cookies, light fruit yogurts, and diet sodas. After arriving at Bronson Alcott High, Tai flirts with Travis as they make their way through the cafeteria lunch line, grimacing at the soggy baked potatoes and steamed broccoli as the lunch lady slops a spoonful of casserole onto the plates. In this chapter, we've transformed those less-than-stellar cafeteria options into munchies (or lunch) like Not-Your-Cafeteria Spicy Baked Potato Wedges (page 35), Better-Than-Bagged Potato Chips (page 29), and Tryin'-to-Be-Healthy Roasted Cauliflower and Broccoli (page 40). Snack on, students!

PRETZEL BITES

¾ cup warm water (105–115°F)

2¼ teaspoons (1 envelope) instant yeast

1 tablespoon firmly packed light brown sugar

2¼ cups (9 ounces) all-purpose flour

½ teaspoon fine sea salt

1 tablespoon unsalted butter, melted

¼ cup baking soda

1 large egg, beaten with 1 teaspoon water, for egg wash

Coarse or flaky sea salt, for sprinkling (optional)

HONEY MUSTARD DIP

3 tablespoons runny honey

3 tablespoons Dijon mustard

2 tablespoons tahini

1 tablespoon grainy mustard

Party in the Valley Pretzel Bites

Big bowls of pretzels and tortilla chips are easy snacks at any party, especially a "rager" in the "Val." Cher, Dionne, and Tai make a cameo at an (oddly) Christmas-themed party, and even though Tai and Travis only seem to have eyes for each other, Cher has other plans: to hook Tai up with Elton. (Of course, Elton is obviously smitten with Cher.) After Tai gets hit in the head with a shoe, Cher manages to get them together on the dance floor and gives herself "snaps" for all the good deeds she is doing. You can easily double the honey mustard dip if you like a lot of sauce. The pretzels are best the day they are made.

To make the pretzel bites: In the bowl of a stand mixer, whisk together with a wire whisk the warm water, yeast, and brown sugar. Add the flour, salt, and melted butter. Mix on low speed, using the dough hook, until the dough comes together, then increase the speed to medium-low and knead until the dough is soft and smooth, about 10 minutes. Remove the bowl from the mixer, cover tightly, and let rise in a warm, draft-free spot until nearly doubled in size, about 1 hour.

Turn the dough out onto a clean work surface and cut into quarters. Roll each quarter of dough into a ¾-inch-thick rope. Cut each rope crosswise into approximately 1-inch lengths. You should have about 44 to 48 dough pieces.

Preheat the oven to 400°F. Line a baking sheet with parchment paper.

Continues on page 22.

In a large saucepan, bring 6 cups of water to a boil. Add the baking soda. Bring to a boil over high heat. In batches, add 10 to 12 of the dough pieces to the boiling water and let boil for 20 seconds. Using a large, slotted spoon or a spider, immediately lift the dough pieces out of the water, letting any excess water drip off. Transfer to the baking sheet. Repeat with all the dough pieces.

Arrange the dough pieces neatly on the baking sheet so they are not touching. Lightly brush the dough pieces with the egg wash, then sprinkle with the coarse or flaky salt (if using). Bake until deep golden brown, about 14 minutes.

To make the honey mustard dip: While the pretzel bites are baking, in a small bowl, whisk together all the ingredients for the honey mustard dip.

Serve the warm pretzel bites with the honey mustard for dipping. Store any leftover bites (as if!) in an airtight container for up to 3 days at room temperature.

15 cups plain, unsalted popcorn (see Note)

2 cups mini pretzels

1 cup roasted, unsalted peanuts

1 cup unsalted butter

2 cups firmly packed light brown sugar

½ cup light corn syrup

½ teaspoon fine sea salt

½ teaspoon baking soda

8 ounces (about 1 heaping cup) candy-coated milk chocolate peanut candies, preferably peanut M&Ms

½ cup chopped red licorice pieces

½ cup mixed chocolate chips

Off-the-Diet Popcorn

This popcorn is everything! Chock-full of pretzels, roasted peanuts, chocolate peanut candies, chocolate chips, and even some licorice, this is one snack that is ready to party. The party-ready nosh is an homage to Cher's snacking confession, "I feel like such a heifer. I had two bowls of Special K, three pieces of turkey bacon, a handful of popcorn, five peanut M&Ms, and like three pieces of licorice."

Note: If you want to pop your own popcorn on the stove, it's easy! Be aware that this can sometimes produce differing yields, depending on the kernels; ½ cup unpopped kernels should yield about 15 cups of popped popcorn. In a large, heavy pot over medium heat, combine 3 tablespoons of avocado or canola oil and 2 kernels of popcorn. Cover and cook until you hear the kernels pop. Remove from the heat and add ½ cup kernels; swirl the pan for about 30 seconds. Cover and continue to cook over medium heat, shaking the pan continuously, until the popping slows to 3 to 5 seconds between pops. Remove the pan from the heat and let sit for 30 seconds, then carefully lift off the lid.

Position 2 racks evenly in the oven and preheat the oven to 250°F. Line 2 large, rimmed baking sheets with parchment paper.

In a large, wide bowl, combine the popcorn, pretzels, and peanuts. Set aside.

Continues on page 26.

To make the caramel coating: In a large saucepan over medium heat, melt the butter. Add the brown sugar, corn syrup, and salt, and cook, stirring constantly, until the mixture comes to a boil. Let boil for about 3 minutes, stirring occasionally. Stir in the baking soda. This makes a smooth caramel.

Working quickly, immediately pour the caramel over the popcorn mixture. Using 2 heatproof spatulas, stir and gently toss until the popcorn mixture is evenly coated all over.

Divide the mixture between the prepared baking sheets and spread in an even layer. Bake for 45 minutes, stirring once or twice and rotating the baking sheets between the racks about halfway through baking. Transfer the pans to a wire rack.

Sprinkle the candies, licorice, and/or chocolate chips over the popcorn. Season with a little more salt while warm, if you like. Let cool completely.

Break into pieces and serve. The popcorn can be stored in airtight containers for up to 5 days at room temperature.

1 small head garlic

Olive oil, for drizzling

¼ cup unsalted butter, at room temperature

Fine sea salt

1 pound store-bought pizza dough

⅓ cup grated Parmesan cheese

½ cup shredded low-moisture mozzarella

So-Cheesy Roasted Garlic Breadsticks

After Cher gives Tai the news that Elton isn't interested in Tai, Cher and Dionne decide to cheer Tai up by going to the mall for a "calorie-fest." "Break me off a piece of that," exclaims Tai as they ogle cute waiters walking by while munching on breadsticks. As Cher and Dionne debate whether they like muscular guys, Tai holds up a crooked breadstick and says, "You know what, I don't really care either way, just as long as his you-know-what isn't crooked."

Preheat the oven to 375°F. Line a large, rimmed baking sheet with parchment paper.

Cut the top ¼ inch off the head of garlic, discarding the top. Drizzle the exposed garlic cloves with a little olive oil. Wrap the head in foil. Bake until the garlic is very soft, about 40 minutes. Open the foil and let cool.

When cool, squeeze the garlic out of the cloves and place in a bowl. Add the butter and a pinch of salt and, using a fork, mash the mixture together.

Increase the oven heat to 400°F.

On a lightly floured surface, roll out the pizza dough into a 10-by-7-inch rectangle. Spread the garlic butter over the dough, all the way to the edges. Sprinkle the Parmesan evenly over the dough, all the way to the edges. Using a pizza cutter or a sharp knife, cut the dough crosswise into ten 1-inch-wide pieces.

Twist each dough rope and arrange on the prepared baking sheet, spacing the dough evenly.

Continues on page 28.

Bake until the breadsticks are lightly golden, about 15 minutes. Remove from the oven and sprinkle evenly with the shredded mozzarella cheese. Return to the oven and bake until the cheese is melted and golden, about 5 to 7 minutes longer. Let cool slightly before serving.

2 quarts ice water

2 tablespoons fine sea salt, plus
more for sprinkling

2 pounds medium russet potatoes,
skin on

Peanut oil or canola oil, for frying

Better-Than-Bagged Potato Chips

Every lunchtime table at Bronson Alcott High School is laden with an array of bagged potato and corn chips produced by every conceivable national brand. Go one step above high school lunch period with these homemade potato chips, and you might just win lunchtime. For the best results, be sure to cut the potato slices thinly and evenly and dry them exceptionally well.

Fill a large bowl with ice and cold water, then stir in the 2 tablespoons salt. Cut the potatoes crosswise into very thin slices, preferably with a mandoline (about $\frac{1}{16}$- to $\frac{1}{8}$-inch thick). Be sure to cut the potato slices as evenly as possible so they fry evenly. Transfer to the bowl of ice water and soak for 30 minutes.

Fill a large, deep, heavy skillet (ideally a 12-inch cast-iron pan that is 3 inches deep) with 1 inch of oil; be sure to not fill the skillet more than halfway full of oil. Warm the oil over medium-high heat to 360–375°F on a deep-frying thermometer.

While the oil is heating, line a baking sheet with paper towels and set near the stovetop.

Drain the potatoes well, discarding any ice. Spread onto paper towels and pat thoroughly dry on both sides.

In batches to avoid crowding, fry the potato slices, turning a few times with tongs or a slotted spoon or wire spider, until golden brown, about 2 minutes.

Transfer to the prepared baking sheet. Sprinkle with salt right away. Repeat to cook all the potato slices.

ROSEMARY FOCACCIA

2 pounds bread flour

3 cups warm water (105–115°F)

1 envelope (2¼ teaspoons) active dry yeast

1 tablespoon honey

1½ tablespoons fine sea salt

1 tablespoon packed minced fresh rosemary

5 to 6 tablespoons extra-virgin olive oil

Flaky salt, for garnish (optional)

ROASTED GARLIC DIPPING OIL

1 small head garlic

½ cup extra-virgin olive oil

Salt and pepper

Family Dinner Rosemary Focaccia

This sumptuous herbed focaccia with roasted garlic oil will feel as at home on your table as it is on Cher's— whether in Beverly Hills or not. But, hopefully, you avoid a contentious grilling like the one Cher's dad gives Josh about his career: When Mel asks Josh if he's given any thought to corporate law, Josh answers that he'd really like to check out environmental law. "What for?" asks Cher's father. "You want to have a miserable, frustrating life?" Cher pipes in, "Oh, Josh will have that no matter what he does."

Note: If you don't want to serve the bread with the dipping oil, you can garnish it with a little more chopped rosemary and some flaky salt just before baking and serve it with plenty of butter.

To make the rosemary focaccia: In a stand mixer fitted with a dough hook, combine the flour and 2½ cups water. Mix on low speed until a rough dough forms. Set the bowl aside, covered, for 30 to 60 minutes.

In a separate bowl, whisk together the yeast, the remaining ½ cup water, and the honey. Set aside until the yeast becomes foamy, about 5 minutes.

Add the yeast mixture to the flour mixture. Return the bowl to the mixer and mix on low speed until the dough comes together. Add the salt and rosemary, and mix on medium speed, until the dough looks elastic, about 5 minutes; it will be very wet and sticky.

Continues on page 32.

Grease a large bowl with 2 tablespoons olive oil, then scrape the dough into the bowl. Turn the dough once or twice to coat with oil. Cover the bowl with an oiled piece of plastic wrap and set in a warm, draft-free spot until the dough doubles in size, about 2 hours.

While the dough rises, make the dipping oil. Preheat the oven to 375°F. Cut the top ¼ inch off the head of garlic, discarding the top. Drizzle the exposed garlic cloves with a little olive oil. Wrap the head in foil. Bake until the garlic is very soft, about 40 to 60 minutes (the timing depends on the garlic!). Open the foil and let cool. When cool, squeeze the garlic out of the cloves and add to a small bowl. Using a fork, mash into a paste, then add the oil and stir until smooth. Season with salt and pepper. (Alternatively, put the roasted garlic and oil in a measuring cup and use an immersion blender to puree the mixture together.) Set aside at room temperature.

Line a large, rimmed baking sheet (about 18 by 13 inches) with parchment paper, then grease the paper and pan sides with 2 tablespoons of oil. Scrape the dough onto the baking sheet and loosely shape it into a rectangle. Cover with the oiled plastic wrap and let it rest for 10 minutes, then uncover and gently stretch the dough to fit the pan in an even layer. If the dough springs back, let it rest for a few more minutes before proceeding.

Drizzle the dough with 1 tablespoon of oil, then set aside, uncovered, to rise until it is puffy and at the height of the pan edges, about 1 to 1½ hours.

Preheat the oven to 450°F.

Dimple the dough all over with your fingertips, pressing to the bottom of the pan. Bake until golden brown, about 20 to 25 minutes. Let cool for 5 minutes, then use a sharp knife to cut around the edges of the focaccia. Slide out of the pan and onto a wire rack, removing the parchment. Let cool before cutting.

Serve pieces of focaccia with the dipping oil alongside.

"

UGH, AS IF

"

Not-Your-Cafeteria Spicy Baked Potato Wedges

SOUR CREAM ONION DIP (MAKES ABOUT 1⅓ CUPS)

1 tablespoon unsalted butter

½ yellow onion, finely chopped

Fine sea salt and freshly ground black pepper

1 cup sour cream

1 teaspoon onion powder

¼ teaspoon garlic powder

¼ teaspoon balsamic vinegar

BAKED POTATO WEDGES

3 tablespoons olive oil

1 teaspoon garlic powder

1 teaspoon smoked paprika

½ teaspoon onion powder

1 teaspoon fine sea salt

½ teaspoon freshly ground black pepper

4 russet potatoes (about 2 pounds)

2 tablespoons chopped fresh flat-leaf parsley, for garnish

Sliding along the Bronson Alcott High School cafeteria lunch line, Tai and Travis strike up a conversation. They quickly connect over their mutual love of art and drawing, and trying to decide between the mediocre baked potatoes, broccoli, and carrots. These spicy baked potato wedges with a creamy onion dip are anything but mediocre. Be sure to choose potatoes that are all about the same size.

To make the onion dip: In a skillet over medium heat, melt the butter. Add the onions and a pinch of salt and cook, stirring, until they start to brown, about 4 minutes. Reduce the heat to low, cover, and cook, stirring occasionally, until caramelized and golden brown, about 10 minutes longer. Transfer to a bowl and let cool completely. Stir in the sour cream, onion powder, garlic powder, and vinegar. Season with salt and pepper.

Meanwhile, position two racks evenly in the oven and preheat to 425°F.

To make the potato wedges: In a bowl, whisk together the oil and spices. Quarter each potato lengthwise, then cut into equal wedges for a total of about 8 wedges per potato. Place the potato wedges in a bowl and drizzle with the oil mixture, tossing to coat evenly.

Divide the potato wedges between two rimmed baking sheets and spread them in a single, even layer so they are not touching. Bake, rotating the pans between racks and turning the potatoes once halfway through, until crisp, golden, and tender, about 30 minutes.

Transfer the hot potato wedges to a platter and garnish with the parsley. Serve with the sour cream dip alongside.

TAHINI-LEMON SAUCE

¼ cup tahini

¼ cup freshly squeezed
lemon juice

2 tablespoons plain yogurt
(not Greek)

1 tablespoon extra-virgin olive oil

¼ teaspoon fine sea salt

SPICY CARROT STICKS

2 tablespoons olive oil

2 cloves garlic, minced

½ teaspoon fine sea salt

¼ teaspoon freshly ground
black pepper

½ teaspoon ground cumin

½ teaspoon sweet paprika

¼ teaspoon ground coriander

¼ teaspoon ground cinnamon

Pinch of cayenne pepper,
or to taste

1 pound medium carrots,
trimmed and peeled

Skinny Spiced Carrot Sticks with Tahini-Lemon Sauce

Cher likes carrot sticks and even keeps a large container of them at the ready for easy munching. As she snacks on them in the kitchen with her stepbrother, Josh goads her for gaining weight, "Oh, wow, you're filling out there." But Cher isn't having it. "Oh, wow, your face is catching up with your mouth," she responds. This tahini-lemon sauce recipe makes more than you need, but it's great on just about everything! Try it on a fresh green salad or as a dip for pita crisps.

Preheat the oven to 450°F.

To make the sauce: In a bowl, whisk together the tahini, lemon juice, yogurt, olive oil, and salt. If the sauce is too thick, add a little water. Cover and refrigerate until ready to use. (The sauce can be made up to 2 days in advance.)

To make the spicy carrot sticks: In a bowl, stir together all the ingredients, except the carrots, until well combined. Cut the carrots in half crosswise, then cut the top halves in half lengthwise. If the bottom halves are thick, you can cut those in half lengthwise as well, but if they are thin, leave them as is so the carrot sticks are all about the same width.

Put the carrots on a large, rimmed baking sheet, add the spice mixture, and toss to coat evenly. Spread into an even layer. Roast the carrots, turning once or twice, until crisp-tender and browned, about 12 to 14 minutes.

Serve warm or at room temperature, drizzled with the sauce. Alternatively, serve the sauce alongside for dipping while fighting with your stepbrother.

Tryin'-to-Be-Healthy
Roasted Cauliflower and Broccoli

RANCH DIP
(MAKES ABOUT 1¼ CUPS)

¼ cup buttermilk

1 teaspoon freshly squeezed lemon juice

1 teaspoon packed minced fresh dill

1 teaspoon packed minced fresh chives

1 teaspoon minced fresh flat-leaf parsley

¼ teaspoon garlic powder

¼ teaspoon onion powder

Fine sea salt

1 cup mayonnaise

ROASTED CAULIFLOWER
AND BROCCOLI

12 ounces cauliflower, cut into 1½-inch florets

1 small crown broccoli (8 ounces), cut into 1½-inch florets

2 tablespoons olive oil

Fine sea salt and freshly ground black pepper

A lot can be said for an active Southern California lifestyle like Cher's, and plenty of fresh vegetables figure into her always-trying-to-be-healthy diet. But healthy doesn't have to equal boring. Roasting cauliflower and broccoli make them majorly, totally better! The vegetables are just fine on their own, but the ranch dip is all that and a bag of chips, so do yourself a favor and take a few extra minutes to make it—plus, it's good on just about everything.

To make the ranch dip: In a blender, combine the buttermilk, lemon juice, herbs, garlic powder, onion powder, and a pinch of salt and blend until smooth. Transfer to a bowl. Add the mayo and whisk until smooth. Cover and refrigerate until ready to use.

To make the roasted cauliflower and broccoli: Preheat the oven to 450°F. Spread the cauliflower and broccoli on a large, rimmed baking sheet, drizzle with the olive oil, then season with salt and pepper. Toss until evenly coated, then spread into an even layer. Roast, turning once, until the vegetables are nicely golden and crisp-tender, about 12 minutes.

Serve warm or at room temperature with the ranch dip alongside for dipping.

2 zucchini (about 1 pound)

Fine sea salt and freshly ground black pepper

Pinch of garlic powder

Avocado or canola oil cooking spray

About ¼ cup grated Parmesan cheese

Snappy Zucchini Parmesan Crisps

These take a couple of hours in the oven, but that leaves you with plenty of time to get a mani-pedi! Also, they are totally healthy—even Cher's dad can eat them on his low-cal diet. Make sure you choose the pre-grated, fine-grained Parmesan—it's drier than freshly grated or shredded and will help keep your chips crispy.

Preheat the oven to 225°F. Slice the zucchini diagonally into ⅛-inch-thick slices. Spread the slices in a single layer on a large baking sheet and sprinkle very lightly with salt, pepper, and garlic powder.

Bake until the zucchini is dry and crisp, about 2 hours. (If you need to divide the zucchini between 2 baking sheets, space the racks evenly in the oven and swap the baking sheets halfway through cooking.)

About 10 minutes before they are done, remove the zucchini from the oven. Spray very lightly with the cooking spray and sprinkle one side with the Parmesan.

Continue baking until the cheese is golden, about 10 minutes longer. Immediately transfer to a wire rack to cool before serving; they will crisp up as they cool. The crisps are best the day they are made, but you can store them in an airtight container at room temperature for up to 3 days.

CRUDITÉS

½ pound medium-thick asparagus spears, trimmed

1 small crown broccoli and/or ½ head cauliflower, cut into 1½-inch florets

8 ounces multicolored baby carrots, halved lengthwise

2 Persian cucumbers, trimmed and cut diagonally into ½-inch slices

½ pound sugar snap peas, trimmed

BAKED BRIE

One 12-ounce round of Brie or Camembert

Gooey Baked Brie with Crudités

Fresh, crunchy veggies like asparagus, sugar snap peas, and cucumbers are the healthier way to scoop up creamy, oozy baked Brie, a much-loved 1990s party appetizer. But toasted baguette slices and crackers would also be fun accessories. To sweeten it up a bit, drizzle the baked Brie with honey right when it comes out of the oven, and it will be as sweet as California sunshine—or Cher and Josh's budding relationship.

Fill a large bowl with ice and cold water. Fill a large saucepan two-thirds full of salted water and bring to a boil over high heat. Blanch the asparagus until just tender and bright green, about 1 minute. Using a slotted spoon or tongs, transfer to the ice bath.

Bring the water back to a boil and add the broccoli and/or cauliflower and cook until just crisp-tender, about 1 minute. Transfer to the ice bath. Drain and pat the vegetables dry with paper towels.

Arrange all the vegetables on a platter large enough to hold them with a space in the center for the Brie.

Preheat the oven to 350°F. Unwrap the Brie and place in an ovenproof ramekin or baking dish just large enough to hold it. (Alternatively, place the Brie on a piece of parchment paper on a small baking sheet or pie pan.) Bake until the Brie is very soft, about 15 to 20 minutes. Transfer to the platter with the veggies and serve at once.

1 teaspoon olive oil

4 ounces small cremini or button mushrooms, trimmed and sliced

Kosher salt and freshly ground black pepper

1 pound store-bought puff pastry

¾ cup (3 ounces) shredded low-moisture mozzarella (not fresh)

2 tablespoons (½ ounce) grated Parmesan

1 large egg, beaten with 1 teaspoon of water, for egg wash

¾ cup of your favorite thick marinara sauce

3 tablespoons pitted sliced black olives

GARLIC BUTTER (OPTIONAL)

1 tablespoon unsalted butter

¼ teaspoon garlic powder

Pinch of fine sea salt

Way Hot Veggie Pizza Pockets

These homemade riffs on the 1990s freezer classic take a bit of precision and a careful hand, but they're way more fun than math class—and they taste far better. They are also endlessly versatile once you get the technique down—swap out diced pepperoni for the mushrooms or make a creamy ham and cheese version with diced ham, bechamel, and shredded Gruyère cheese. You'll want to use a thick, smooth tomato sauce for this recipe, not anything watery or chunky.

To make the pizza pockets: In a medium skillet over medium heat, warm the oil. Add the mushrooms, season with salt and pepper, and cook, stirring occasionally, until tender and they have released their liquid, about 5 minutes. Set aside to cool completely.

Line a baking sheet with parchment paper. Roll out the puff-pastry dough into a rectangle that measures 20 by 10 inches and is about ⅛-inch thick. Trim any uneven edges. Cut into twelve 5-by-4-inch rectangles (a ruler and pizza wheel make this easier). Transfer to the baking sheet and refrigerate for 15 minutes.

In a bowl, toss together the mozzarella and Parmesan.

Continues on page 48.

Make each pizza pocket one at a time, leaving the remaining puff-pastry rectangles in the refrigerator to stay cold. Remove 2 rectangles of puff pastry at a time, and place on a lightly floured work surface. Gently roll the dough out again to the original dimensions (5 by 4 inches) if it has shrunk slightly after being chilled. Brush 1 puff rectangle around the edges lightly with the egg wash (covering at least ½ inch).

In the center of the rectangle, leaving a ½-inch border all the way around, layer 1 scant tablespoon sauce, 1 tablespoon cheese mixture, 1 tablespoon mushrooms, ½ tablespoon olives, 1 scant tablespoon sauce, and 1 tablespoon of the cheese mixture. Top with another puff-pastry rectangle, gently stretching it over the filling to reach the edges of the puff rectangle on the bottom and firmly pressing around the edges while expelling any air and keeping the filling inside. Use the pizza wheel to trim the edges, if needed, making sure you don't cut near the filling. Crimp lightly with a fork. Return to the refrigerator and repeat to create the remaining pizza pockets. Refrigerate for 15 minutes.

Meanwhile, preheat the oven to 375°F. Pierce the pockets a few times on top. Brush lightly with the egg wash. Bake until golden brown and puffed, about 20 minutes. Serve right away.

To make the garlic butter: If you like, while the pizza pockets are baking, in a small skillet, melt the butter. Add the garlic powder and salt, and stir to combine. Set aside. When the pizza pockets are ready, brush the tops gently with the garlic butter.

"TOTAL BETTY"

CHAPTER THREE
Not-Your-School-Cafeteria Lunches

Lunch doesn't have to be a prepackaged container of pasta salad, a candy bar, or the slop from the school cafeteria. With plenty of 1990s attitude and in celebration of Cher's love of makeovers, we transformed Josh's slapped-together turkey-and-white-bread sandwich into Makeover Turkey Sandwiches (page 54). You might also get on board with the Total Betty Turkey "Bacon Experience" BLTAs (page 58) or a zingy Teachers' Lounge Italian Tuna Pasta Salad (page 64). And if you're feeling a little "bratty" after your stepbrother has been getting under your skin while chomping pickles straight out of the jar, the Bratty Egg Salad Sandwiches with Quick Dill Pickles (page 62) might be just the ticket.

Makeover Turkey Sandwiches

3 tablespoons mayonnaise or aioli

2 tablespoons sun-dried-tomato pesto

4 slices rustic whole-wheat or sourdough bread

3 to 4 ounces thinly sliced smoked or roasted turkey

2 slices provolone cheese

2 small jarred roasted red bell peppers, drained and sliced

2 to 3 tablespoons sliced pepperoncini

4 thin slices ripe tomato

Handful of fresh baby spinach leaves (about ¼ cup)

Sometimes your turkey sandwich, like your friend, needs a makeover. As Josh slaps together slices of white bread and turkey right out of the refrigerator, Cher vows to him that she's going to make Tai well-dressed and popular and that Tai's life will be better because of her. "How many girls can say that about you?" Much like Tai's makeover, we've given Josh's sad turkey sandwich a California update—a masterpiece that will take your new friend (or your lunch box) by storm. Creamy sun-dried-tomato-pesto mayonnaise, roasted red bell peppers, zingy pepperoncini, fresh ripe tomato, and baby spinach elevate this to an exceptional sandwich. What's not to love?

In a bowl, stir together the mayonnaise and pesto. Spread the mayonnaise on one side of each slice of bread.

On 2 of the bread slices, layer the turkey, cheese, roasted peppers, pepperoncini, tomato slices, and spinach on top, dividing the ingredients evenly. Lay a bread slice, mayonnaise side down, on top of the sandwich. Cut it in half if you like and serve.

BALSAMIC VINAIGRETTE

⅓ cup extra-virgin olive oil

3 tablespoons balsamic vinegar

1 teaspoon grainy mustard,
or to taste

Fine sea salt and freshly ground
black pepper

SALAD

¼ cup pine nuts

6 cups mixed lettuces

¼ cup finely chopped sun-dried
tomatoes

Mixed Greens Salad Forever!

No 1990s recipe collection would be complete without a simple mixed greens salad. In fact, you'll see a salad in practically every lunch or dinner scene in *Clueless*. Topped off with lightly toasted pine nuts, tangy and chewy sun-dried tomatoes, and a sweet balsamic vinaigrette, this simple salad is "da bomb" and epitomizes popular ingredients from the '90s.

To make the vinaigrette: Combine the oil, vinegar, and mustard in a small jar with a tight-fitting lid. Season with salt and pepper. Tighten the lid and shake vigorously until emulsified. Set aside.

To make the salad: In a small skillet over medium-low heat, toast the pine nuts, gently swirling the pan occasionally, until fragrant and golden, about 5 minutes. Transfer to a plate and let cool completely.

In a medium bowl, toss the lettuce with a few tablespoons of the vinaigrette. Divide the lettuces between 4 individual plates. Sprinkle with the pine nuts and sun-dried tomatoes, and drizzle with a little more vinaigrette. Serve, passing any remaining vinaigrette at the table.

Total Betty Turkey "Bacon Experience" BLTAs

1 tablespoon avocado or canola oil

6 slices turkey bacon

1 small ripe avocado, pitted, peeled, and sliced

4 slices rustic whole-wheat or sourdough bread, lightly toasted

2 tablespoons garlic aioli or mayonnaise

4 thick slices ripe heirloom tomato

2 to 4 romaine heart leaves or butter lettuce leaves

The early 1990s saw the beginning of the low-fat food craze, and everything from cookies to bacon was fair game for a low-fat makeover. This era is also when turkey bacon joined the American mainstream, with promises of low-calorie health benefits while still delivering the "bacon experience." Make sure your BLTA is a "total Betty"—just like Cher's mom—by choosing the best-quality ingredients: ripe heirloom tomato; artisan wheat bread; and a good-quality, organic turkey bacon made from dark-meat turkey. And don't skimp on cooking the bacon in a little fat—the results are well worth it.

In a large skillet over medium-low heat, warm the oil. Add the bacon and fry, turning once, until crisp, about 7 to 9 minutes. Drain on paper towels.

Divide the avocado slices between 2 of the bread slices. Using a fork, mash the avocado into an even layer. Spread the aioli or mayonnaise on one side of each of the other 2 slices of bread.

Arrange the turkey bacon on top of the avocado, dividing it evenly, then top with the tomato slices and lettuce. Place the other bread slices, mayonnaise side down, on top of the sandwich. Cut it in half if you like and serve.

1 small red bell pepper, seeded and cut into strips

1 small green bell pepper, seeded and cut into strips

1 small yellow onion, halved and sliced

Olive oil

Fine sea salt and freshly ground black pepper

4 fresh Italian pork sausages or bratwurst (about 1 pound total)

4 small hoagie rolls

Stone-ground mustard, for serving

Chopped fresh flat-leaf parsley, for garnish (optional)

Festival Sausage Sandwiches

The cheery atmosphere of Travis's beachside skateboarding competition is the backdrop for Tai and Cher to rekindle their friendship and apologize to each other for fighting. It's a festive day with coffee, a sausage sandwich stand, and watching the sparks ignite between Tai and Travis. Once Cher realizes that Tai and Travis are an item, it becomes clear that Josh is now "out of the picture" for Tai. These Italian sausage sandwiches are topped with plenty of peppers and onions and would make a worthy appearance at any event, skateboards or not.

Preheat a grill for direct cooking over medium heat. Brush the grill grates clean. Place a perforated grill pan on the grill to preheat for about 10 minutes.

Combine the bell peppers and onions in a bowl, and drizzle with a little olive oil. Season with salt and pepper and toss to combine. Spread into an even layer on the grill pan and cook, stirring a few times, until crisp-tender and starting to char a bit, about 7 minutes. Remove from the grill (or slide over to indirect heat).

Rub the sausages lightly with oil. Grill over direct heat for 4 minutes on one side, or until the sausages release from the grate and have grill marks. Continue to cook, turning once or twice, until nicely seared on two sides and cooked through but juicy, about 4 to 7 minutes longer. During the last few minutes of cooking, toast the rolls, cut sides down.

To assemble: Spread each roll with mustard, then top with a sausage and a quarter of the pepper mixture. Garnish with parsley, if you like, and serve.

QUICK DILL PICKLES

4 small Persian cucumbers, trimmed and quartered lengthwise (each no longer than 4 inches)

2 sprigs fresh dill

1 clove garlic

⅔ cup water

½ cup distilled white vinegar

1 teaspoon granulated sugar

½ teaspoon mustard seeds

¼ teaspoon fine sea salt

EGG SALAD SANDWICHES

6 large eggs

¼ cup mayonnaise

1 small stalk celery, finely chopped

1 green onion, white and green parts, finely chopped

1 tablespoon finely chopped fresh herbs, loosely packed, such as flat-leaf parsley, chives, and/or dill

½ teaspoon finely grated lemon zest

½ teaspoon freshly squeezed lemon juice

Fine sea salt and freshly ground black pepper

8 slices white or whole-wheat bread

4 butter lettuce leaves

Bratty Egg Salad Sandwiches with Quick Dill Pickles

Cher is not having it when Tai starts to become more popular than her. In an angry fit, she throws around a pile of clothes in her room, then yells at and insults her housekeeper. Josh, meanwhile, looks on, eating pickles straight from the jar. He tells Cher she's "such a brat" as she storms from the room on her way to her driving test. This herb-packed egg sandwich, kissed with lemon, is certain to be a popular addition to your lunchtime routine, especially when paired with couldn't-be-easier homemade dill pickles.

To make the pickles: Pack the cucumber spears, dill, and garlic clove into a pint-sized, wide-mouth jar with a screw-top lid (a mason jar works well) and refrigerate. In a small saucepan over medium heat, combine the water, vinegar, sugar, mustard seeds, and salt, stirring just until the sugar dissolves. Remove from the heat and set aside to cool to room temperature. Pour the mixture over the cucumbers. It should come to the top of the jar; if not, add enough water to cover. Cover and refrigerate for at least 1 hour, or up to 2 weeks.

To make the egg salad: Fill a bowl with ice water and set aside. Fill a saucepan with about 1 inch of water and fit a steamer insert over the top. Bring the water to a boil over high heat. Add the eggs in an even layer and cover the pan. Cook for 12 minutes. Transfer to the ice water and let cool for at least 10 minutes.

When cool, peel the eggs and transfer to a cutting board. Chop the eggs and transfer to a medium bowl. Add the mayonnaise, celery, green onion, herbs, lemon zest, and lemon juice. Using a fork, stir to combine well. Taste and season with salt and pepper.

Divide the egg salad between 4 pieces of bread. Top each with a lettuce leaf and another piece of bread. Serve with the pickle spears alongside.

Teachers' Lounge Italian Tuna Pasta Salad

Fine sea salt and freshly ground black pepper

12 ounces small pasta shapes, such as fusilli, cavatelli, or penne

⅓ cup plus 1 teaspoon extra-virgin olive oil

2 ears corn on the cob, husks and silk removed

½ cup sliced or chopped pitted black olives, such as kalamata

2 cups halved cherry tomatoes

2 tablespoons red wine vinegar, or to taste

2 tablespoons freshly squeezed lemon juice, or to taste

14 to 16 ounces (2 to 3 jars or cans) good-quality tuna, preferably packed in olive oil, drained

3 tablespoons finely chopped fresh flat-leaf parsley

4 ounces crumbled feta cheese

Lunch in the high school teachers' lounge is a hodgepodge of sandwiches, chips, muffins, juice boxes, diet soda, candy bars, and this classic Italian American tricolored corkscrew pasta salad with olives and vinaigrette. As Cher tries desperately to think of a way to get her teacher, Mr. Hall, to change her grade in her debate class, she scans the teachers' lounge and realizes that all she needs to do to get a better grade is make Mr. Hall sublimely happy. Her eyes fall on Miss Geist, and her grand scheme to fix up Mr. Hall and Miss Geist begins.

Bring a large pot of salted water to a boil over high heat. Add the pasta and cook until al dente, or according to package directions. Drain in a colander, rinsing well under cold water. Transfer to a large serving bowl.

Heat a large, cast-iron pan over medium-high heat until very hot. Add the 1 teaspoon oil and the corn cobs and roast, turning a few times, until nicely browned and crisp-tender, about 5 minutes. Transfer to a cutting board. When cool enough to handle, cut the kernels from the cob.

Add the corn kernels, olives, and tomatoes to the pasta. Drizzle with the ⅓ cup olive oil, vinegar, and lemon juice and toss to combine. Crumble the tuna over the pasta and add the parsley and feta. Toss gently to combine. Season to taste with salt, pepper, and/or more vinegar or lemon juice. Serve. The pasta salad can be stored in an airtight container in the refrigerator for up to 3 days.

CITRUS VINAIGRETTE

¼ cup extra-virgin olive oil

¼ cup avocado oil

½ teaspoon finely grated orange zest

3 tablespoons fresh orange juice

2 tablespoons freshly squeezed lemon juice

1 teaspoon white wine vinegar or rice vinegar

1 teaspoon minced shallot

½ teaspoon honey (optional)

Fine sea salt and freshly ground black pepper

Continues on page 68.

So-Lo-Cal Chopped Chicken, Avocado, and Herb Salad

Head down the lunch line on any given day and you'll be able to find cooked chicken breast on offer. In true *Clueless* fashion, Dionne asks Cher, "Are you sure that's fat-free?" "Oh, yes," Cher replies as she digs into a chicken breast, "and you lose weight by [cutting it into tiny pieces]." This fabulous SoCal-inspired salad—filled with creamy avocado, fresh cherry tomatoes, cucumber, plenty of herbs, and a tangy citrus vinaigrette—is a significant improvement on school cafeteria fare and would surely get Dionne and Cher's approval. Throw in a can of drained chickpeas and some diced fresh mozzarella or provolone to boost the heartiness of this salad.

To make the vinaigrette: Combine the oils, citrus zest and juices, vinegar, shallot, and honey (if using) in a small jar with a tight-fitting lid. Season with salt and pepper. Tighten the lid and shake vigorously until emulsified.

To make the chicken salad: Lightly pound each chicken breast to an even thickness (around ¾ to 1 inch). Season the chicken with salt and pepper, place in a shallow baking dish, and drizzle with ¼ cup of the vinaigrette. Refrigerate for at least 30 minutes or up to 2 hours to marinate.

Continues on page 68.

CHICKEN SALAD

1 pound boneless skinless chicken breasts

Fine sea salt and freshly ground black pepper

2 hearts of romaine lettuce, chopped (about 6 cups)

1 cup halved grape or cherry tomatoes

1 Persian cucumber or ½ small English cucumber, diced

2 semi-firm but ripe small avocados, peeled, pitted, and diced

½ small red onion, very thinly sliced

2 tablespoons (loosely packed) roughly chopped mixed fresh herbs, such as flat-leaf parsley, chives, basil, tarragon, mint leaves, and/or dill

Preheat a gas or charcoal grill for direct grilling over medium heat (about 400°F). Brush the grill grates clean. Remove the chicken from the marinade, letting any excess marinade drip off. Grill the chicken, with the lid closed, until it releases easily from the grates, about 4 minutes. Turn and grill the other side until opaque all the way through, about 4 minutes. Set aside to cool for at least 10 minutes. Chop the chicken into bite-size pieces.

In a large, wide salad bowl, toss together the lettuce, tomatoes, cucumber, avocados, red onion, and herbs. Add the chicken and ¼ cup of the vinaigrette and toss to coat evenly. Serve, passing the remaining dressing alongside.

Totally Not Buggin' Baked Goat Cheese Salad with Herb Vinaigrette and Crostini

HERB VINAIGRETTE (MAKES ½ CUP)

1 tablespoon packed finely chopped mixed fresh herbs, such as flat-leaf parsley, chives, basil, tarragon, mint leaves, and/or dill

⅓ cup extra-virgin olive oil

2 tablespoons freshly squeezed lemon juice, or to taste

1 tablespoon rice vinegar or white wine vinegar

1 teaspoon Dijon mustard, or to taste

½ teaspoon honey, or to taste

Fine sea salt and freshly ground black pepper

CROSTINI

Eight ½-inch-thick slices baguette, cut on the diagonal

About 1 tablespoon olive oil

1 clove garlic, peeled and halved

BAKED GOAT CHEESE

½ cup panko or fine dried breadcrumbs

8 ounces fresh goat cheese

Olive oil, for brushing

6 cups mixed greens

This is the ultimate sit-down dinner party salad. It looks so pretty on a plate with the breadcrumb–coated baked goat cheese disks and crunchy crostini—and it's so easy that even Cher could make it. Just make sure you ask your guests to RSVP so you know how much salad to make (it's easily doubled or tripled!), or you might get stuck improvising, as Cher did: "It's like, when I had this garden party for my father's birthday, I said RSVP because it was a sit-down dinner, but people came that did not, like, RSVP, so I was like, totally buggin'."

To make the vinaigrette: Place the herbs in a blender, then add the oil, lemon juice, vinegar, Dijon mustard, and honey. Blend until well combined. Season with salt and pepper. Adjust to taste with more lemon juice, Dijon, or honey, if you like. Transfer to a bowl.

To make the crostini: Preheat the oven to 400°F. Arrange the baguette slices in a single layer on a baking sheet. Brush with oil on both sides. Bake, turning once, until golden brown, about 8 minutes. Rub the warm crostini on one side with the garlic clove halves. Set aside to cool.

Continues on page 72.

To make the baked goat cheese: Place a small baking sheet in the oven to preheat. Put the breadcrumbs into a shallow bowl. Divide the goat cheese into 8 equal pieces and shape each into a disk about ½ inch thick. Brush the goat cheese disks all over with olive oil, then press each disk into the breadcrumbs to coat on both sides and the edges. Remove the baking sheet and brush with 1 tablespoon oil. Arrange the disks in an even layer on the baking sheet. Bake until the bottom is golden and the cheese is lightly bubbling, about 6 to 9 minutes. Let cool on the pan for 10 minutes (this will help the cheese set up).

To assemble: In a medium bowl, toss the lettuce with a few tablespoons of the vinaigrette. Divide the lettuce between 4 individual plates. Top each with 2 of the baked goat cheese disks, browned side up, and drizzle with a little more vinaigrette. Arrange 2 crostini on each plate. Serve, passing any remaining vinaigrette at the table.

Sweet and Sour Teens
Ginger Chicken Salad

**SWEET AND SOUR
GINGER DRESSING**

3 tablespoons avocado oil or
canola oil

3 tablespoons rice vinegar

2 tablespoons reduced-sodium
tamari or soy sauce

1 tablespoon toasted sesame oil

1 teaspoon peeled and finely
grated fresh ginger

1 teaspoon toasted sesame seeds

1½ teaspoons granulated sugar,
or to taste

1 small clove garlic, minced

½ teaspoon freshly ground
black pepper

Continues on next page.

This popular 1990s salad—dubiously named Chinese Chicken Salad (despite not being related to Chinese cuisine)—was a smash hit in California and is an example of the Americanized "fusion" cuisine that swept the nation during that time. Two kinds of crunchy cabbage, sweet carrots and red bell peppers, roasted cashews, and an extra-flavor-packed sesame-ginger dressing make this salad still hella good. Add edamame or blanched broccoli florets, if you like, or toss in cooked rice noodles. If you like a lot of dressing, you can easily double the recipe. It's great on noodles, too!

To make the dressing: In a jar with a tight-fitting lid, place all the ingredients. Shake vigorously to blend. Set aside.

To make the salad: In a large bowl, toss together the napa cabbage, red cabbage, chicken, carrots, bell peppers, green onions, cashews, and cilantro. Drizzle with as much dressing as you like and toss to coat evenly. Divide between bowls and garnish with the chow mein noodles and sesame seeds. Serve at once.

CHICKEN SALAD

3 cups finely shredded napa cabbage (about 5 ounces)

2 cups loosely packed finely shredded red cabbage (about 5 ounces)

2 cups packed cooked shredded chicken breast (about ½ pound)

½ cup finely shredded carrots (about 2 carrots)

½ red bell pepper, seeded and cut crosswise into strips

4 green onions, white and green parts, thinly sliced

¼ cup chopped roasted cashews or peanuts

¼ cup chopped fresh cilantro

1 cup canned crunchy chow mein noodles or fried wonton strips

1 tablespoon toasted sesame seeds, for garnish

"OOPS, MY BAD"

CHAPTER FOUR
Awkward Family Dinners

"We're going to have a nice family dinner!" Cher's father barks at her as she tries to answer Dionne's page. Dinnertime is one of the only times Cher gets to check in with her father, even if the effort is momentary before Daddy answers a work call and starts yelling into his cordless phone. While her father would rather have a thick steak, Cher is often looking out for his health. She follows the advice of his doctor, serving Cut-Your-Cholesterol Salmon and Spring Vegetable Fettuccine (page 92), roasted asparagus (try the Chuckleheads Asparagus Quiche on page 84), and always a simple mixed greens salad (like the Mixed Greens Salad Forever! on page 57). When work gets extra busy and the family can't gather around the dining room table, Cher and Josh bond over getting late-night take-out burgers (make your own with the Midnight Snack Burgers on page 88). California Healthy Veggie Burgers (page 99) would also be "totally dope."

As If! Crab Cakes with Mango Salsa

MANGO SALSA

1 cup diced fresh mango
(about 1 large mango)

¼ cup finely chopped red bell
pepper (about ¼ large pepper)

3 tablespoons finely chopped
red onion

3 tablespoons finely chopped
fresh cilantro

Juice of 1 lime, or to taste

Fine sea salt

CRAB CAKES

1 large egg, beaten

¼ cup mayonnaise

1½ tablespoons finely chopped
red bell pepper

1 tablespoon minced fresh chives

1 teaspoon Dijon mustard

1 teaspoon Worcestershire sauce

1 pound cooked lump crabmeat,
picked over for shells

1 cup fresh breadcrumbs, divided

Fine sea salt and freshly ground
black pepper

¼ cup olive oil

Crab cakes might have initially been popularized on the East Coast, but in the 1990s, they went nationwide. This version mashes up another popular 1990s condiment— mango salsa—for a fresh, healthy, decidedly Californian take. The mango salsa is not only great on crab cakes, but also on grilled fish or chicken, or just with tortilla chips! Choose a fragrant mango that is ripe but still a little firm.

To make the salsa: In a bowl, stir together the mango, bell pepper, red onion, and cilantro. Stir in the lime juice and season with salt. Set aside.

To make the crab cakes: Line a small baking sheet with parchment paper. In a large bowl, whisk together the egg, mayonnaise, bell pepper, chives, mustard, and Worcestershire sauce until smooth. Gently stir in the crabmeat and half of the breadcrumbs. Scoop up about 2 heaping tablespoons of the mixture and press into a cake about ¾ inch thick and 2½ inches in diameter. Transfer to the baking sheet and repeat to make 12 cakes. (Cook right away or cover and refrigerate until ready to fry; the cakes can be made up to 3 hours in advance.)

In a large skillet over medium-low heat, warm the oil. Put the remaining ½ cup breadcrumbs onto a plate and lightly coat both sides of each crab cake. In batches, fry the crab cakes, turning once, until golden brown on both sides, about 3 minutes. Transfer to a paper towel–lined plate to drain. Serve at once with the salsa.

9-inch unbaked pie shell, store-bought (or make your own pie dough using the Tai Lattice Peach Pie recipe on page 115)

10 ounces medium asparagus

4 large eggs

1 cup half-and-half or ½ cup whole milk and ½ cup heavy whipping cream

Fine sea salt and freshly ground black pepper

2 green onions, trimmed and thinly sliced

1 tablespoon finely chopped flat-leaf parsley leaves or fresh tarragon or a mix

3 ounces crumbled feta cheese

Chuckleheads Asparagus Quiche

Dinner with Cher's dad and stepbrother is always a delightful experience, as they throw insults and barbs across the table. At least the food is appealing, whether it's fresh asparagus, a big mixed greens salad (see page 57), or homemade focaccia (see page 30). But make sure you are on time, or Dad will get after you. "Come on, you chuckleheads, get in here!" yells Cher's dad. "Josh, are you still growing?" he asks, then pointedly looks at Cher before saying, "Doesn't he look bigger?" To which Cher replies, "His head does!"

If you're using homemade pie dough, roll out the dough and line a 9-inch pie pan. Freeze the crust for at least 30 minutes (or up to 1 month in advance, wrapped).

Position a rack in the lower third of the oven and preheat to 400°F.

Line the pie shell with parchment paper and fill with pie weights (dried beans or uncooked rice work well). Partially bake the homemade piecrust until the crust looks dry, about 20 minutes. Carefully remove the parchment and pie weights. Continue to bake until lightly golden, about 5 minutes longer. Set aside to cool. (If using a store-bought crust, follow the directions on the packaging to partially bake the pie shell.)

Continues on page 86.

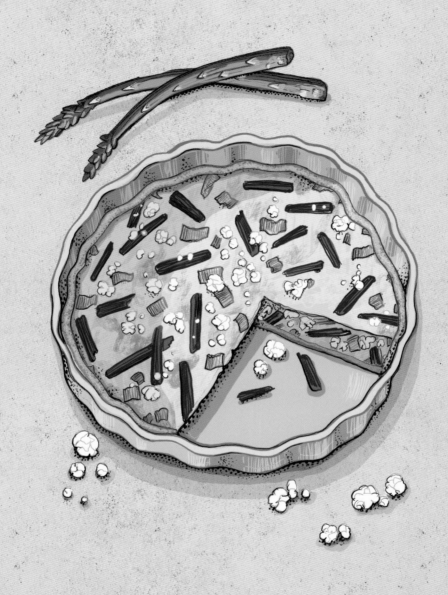

Meanwhile, snap the woody ends off the asparagus and cut crosswise into ½-inch pieces. (You should have about 2 cups.) Fill a medium bowl with ice and cold water. Bring a saucepan half full of salted water to a boil over high heat. Add the asparagus and cook for 1 minute. Drain, then immediately transfer to the ice water to stop the cooking. Let sit for 5 minutes, then drain well.

In a bowl, whisk together the eggs, half-and-half, ½ teaspoon salt, and a few grinds of pepper. Sprinkle the asparagus, green onions, and herbs in an even layer into the pie shell. Pour the egg mixture over the vegetables, then sprinkle the feta over the top.

Reduce the oven temperature to 375°F. Bake until the filling is set, about 45 minutes. Let cool for 15 minutes on a wire rack before slicing and serving.

"WHATEVER!"

Midnight Snack Burgers

When Cher's dad is working on a big case, she and Josh bring the lawyers a "midnight snack" of coffee, bags of potato and corn chips, and plenty of burgers and fries. The midnight snack totally revives the lawyers, and Daddy is grateful, although Cher won't let her dad eat the burger and instead tries to get him to eat fruit and salad. If you're up late, working on an important case, this tasty burger— with homemade "special sauce"—is just the ticket to get you through the wee hours of the night.

SPECIAL SAUCE

¼ cup mayonnaise

2 tablespoons ketchup

1 tablespoon minced bread and butter pickles or sweet pickle relish

2 teaspoons Dijon or yellow mustard

½ teaspoon apple cider vinegar

½ teaspoon sweet paprika

Freshly ground black pepper

BURGERS

2 tablespoons minced yellow onion

2 teaspoons Dijon or yellow mustard

2 teaspoons Worcestershire sauce

1⅓ pounds ground chuck or sirloin

Fine sea salt and freshly ground black pepper

4 slices Cheddar cheese (4 ounces total)

4 sesame burger buns, split

TOPPINGS (OPTIONAL)

Bread and butter or dill pickle slices

4 thin slices red onion

4 thin slices ripe, fresh tomato

4 crunchy lettuce leaves

To make the sauce: In a bowl, stir together all the ingredients. Refrigerate until ready to use.

To make the burgers: In a bowl, whisk together the onion, mustard, and Worcestershire sauce. Add the beef, ½ teaspoon of salt, and ¼ teaspoon of pepper and, using your hands, gently mix the onion mixture into the beef.

Divide the beef mixture into 4 equal portions and gently form into patties, each about 4 inches wide and ¾ inch thick. Loosely cover the meat and let it come to room temperature, about 20 minutes. Meanwhile, prepare a grill for direct cooking over high heat (450–550°F).

Grill the patties, turning once, until done the way you like them, about 7 minutes total for medium-rare. Lay a slice of cheese on each burger, cover the grill, and cook until the cheese is melted, about 30 seconds. Transfer the patties to a plate.

Continues on page 90.

Toast the buns, cut side down on the grill, then transfer to the plate.

To assemble the burgers: Spread the sauce on the cut sides of the buns. Top the bottom bun with a burger patty and the toppings of your choice. Cap it off with the top half of the bun and eat right away.

Note: For thinner burgers, use 1 pound of ground beef and shape into ½-inch-thick patties; reduce the cooking time slightly for medium-rare.

Cut-Your-Cholesterol Salmon and Spring Vegetable Fettuccine

Fine sea salt and freshly ground black pepper

10 ounces medium-thick asparagus spears, trimmed of woody ends and cut into ½-inch pieces

6-ounce jar marinated artichoke hearts

1 pound dried fettuccine

4 tablespoons olive oil

1 pound salmon fillet, pin bones removed

1 small leek, halved lengthwise and thinly sliced

6 ounces sugar snap peas, trimmed and cut into ¼-inch pieces on the diagonal

2 tablespoons chopped fresh flat-leaf parsley, plus more for garnish

1 tablespoon chopped fresh chives, plus more for garnish

1 tablespoon chopped fresh tarragon, plus more for garnish

2 tablespoons freshly squeezed lemon juice

Lemon wedges, for serving

Freshly grated Parmesan, for topping (optional)

Crusty bread, for serving

Cher introduces her dad to Tai as they sit down to dinner together. As her father looks skeptically at Tai, he snaps, "Get out of my chair," before looking at the bowl of pasta and exclaiming, "What is this crap?!" Cher explains, "Daddy, it's from the *Cut Your Cholesterol* cookbook. Dr. Lovett says you've got to get down to 200." Whether you're looking for a healthy dinner option or you just like fresh vegetables, you're in for a treat with this herb-and-lemon-infused pasta with pan-seared salmon.

Fill a medium bowl with ice and cold water. Bring a large saucepan half full of salted water to a boil over high heat. Add the asparagus and cook for 1 minute. Drain, then immediately transfer to the ice water to stop the cooking. Let sit for 5 minutes, then drain well. Drain the artichoke hearts, reserving the liquid, then chop the artichoke hearts.

Fill the large saucepan two-thirds full of salted water and bring to a boil over high heat. Add the pasta and cook until al dente, about 8 minutes, or according to the package directions. Drain, reserving ½ cup of the pasta water.

While the pasta is cooking, in a large skillet over medium-high heat, warm 2 tablespoons of oil. Season the salmon with salt and pepper, then place the salmon, skin side up, in the hot pan. Sear until the salmon is golden brown and releases easily from the pan, about 4 minutes. Turn and continue cooking to medium, about 3 minutes longer. Transfer to a plate. When cool enough to handle, remove and discard the skin and break up the salmon into bite-size pieces.

Continues on page 94.

Wipe out the skillet and place over medium-low heat. Add the remaining olive oil. Add the leek, season with salt, and cook, stirring, until wilted, about 2 minutes. Add the reserved asparagus and sugar snap peas, and stir until warmed and tender, about 3 minutes. Stir in the artichoke hearts, parsley, chives, and tarragon. Stir in about ¼ cup of the reserved pasta cooking water, the lemon juice, and a few tablespoons of the reserved artichoke heart marinade. Add the pasta and toss well, then gently stir in the cooked salmon. Add more pasta water if the pasta seems dry.

Serve in shallow bowls with the lemon wedges alongside, garnished with herbs. If you like, top each serving with freshly grated Parmesan and serve with crusty bread.

2 tablespoons avocado oil

1 small yellow onion, finely chopped

2 medium stalks celery, finely chopped

1 small red bell pepper, seeded and finely chopped

½ green bell pepper, seeded and finely chopped

Fine sea salt

1½ pounds ground beef

¾ cup ketchup

½ cup tomato sauce

2 tablespoons country Dijon or brown mustard

2 tablespoons Worcestershire sauce

1 tablespoon firmly packed light brown sugar

1 tablespoon apple cider vinegar

½ teaspoon freshly ground black pepper

¼ teaspoon red pepper flakes (optional)

6 sesame or brioche burger buns, split and toasted

Slam-Dunk Sloppy Joes

Sloppy joes might be old-fashioned, but they remain a popular comfort food even today. They're also a favorite choice for lunch in the high school teachers' lounge, especially with the PE teacher, who, to Cher's amusement, launches an empty yogurt carton across the lounge and into the trash. Her hoagie-sized sloppy joe is a slam-dunk lunch or dinner, especially when you are looking for something hearty. Top each sandwich with slices of Cheddar or American cheese, if you like.

In a large sauté pan over medium-high heat, warm the oil. Add the onion, celery, and red and green bell peppers. Season with salt. Cook, stirring, until the vegetables are tender and starting to brown, about 8 minutes. Crumble the beef into the pan and cook, stirring and breaking up the beef, until browned, about 5 minutes.

Stir in ¼ cup water, the ketchup, tomato sauce, mustard, Worcestershire sauce, brown sugar, vinegar, ½ teaspoon of salt, pepper, and red pepper flakes (if using), and bring to a simmer. Reduce the heat to low and simmer, stirring often, until the flavors are blended and the mixture thickens slightly, about 20 minutes.

To serve, top the bun bottoms with the sloppy joe mixture, dividing it equally. Cover with the bun tops and serve at once.

Grade-Changing Grilled Spinach Pesto Chicken Breasts

SPINACH-BASIL PESTO (MAKES ABOUT 1 CUP)

1 to 2 cloves garlic, finely chopped

3 ounces packed baby spinach leaves (about 2 cups)

1 cup packed fresh basil leaves (about 1¼ ounces)

⅓ cup extra-virgin olive oil

¼ cup grated Parmesan cheese

1 tablespoon freshly squeezed lemon juice

¼ teaspoon fine sea salt

¼ teaspoon freshly ground black pepper

GRILLED CHICKEN

4 boneless skinless chicken breasts (each about 6 ounces)

Fine sea salt and freshly ground black pepper

Cher, her dad, and her stepbrother, Josh, are sitting around the dinner table. When her dad asks about her report card, Cher replies that it's not ready yet. Confused, her dad asks for an explanation. "Well, some teachers were trying to lowball me, Daddy. And I know how you say never accept a first offer, so I figure these grades are just a jumping-off point to start negotiations." After Josh calls her a "superficial space cadet," he asks what makes her think she can get teachers to change her grades. "Only the fact that I've done it every other semester," Cher retorts. This nut-free, spinach-based pesto will earn top grades at the dinner table and tastes great on everything, from pasta to grilled chicken breasts or salmon.

To make the pesto: In a blender or food processor, combine the garlic, spinach, basil, olive oil, Parmesan, lemon juice, salt, and pepper. Blend, stopping once or twice to scrape down the sides with a rubber spatula, then continuing to blend until smooth. Taste and season with more salt, pepper, or lemon juice, as you like. Transfer to a bowl, press a piece of plastic wrap directly on the surface, and refrigerate until ready to use, up to 3 days in advance. (If you like, freeze the pesto in small airtight containers or ice cube trays; defrost completely before using.)

Continues on page 98.

Lightly pound each chicken breast to an even thickness (around ¾ inch). Season the chicken with salt and pepper and place in a shallow baking dish. Rub each breast all over with about 2 teaspoons of the pesto (2 to 3 tablespoons total). Cover and refrigerate for 30 minutes or up to 2 hours.

Preheat a gas or charcoal grill for direct grilling over medium heat (about 400°F). Brush the grill grates clean. Grill the chicken, with the lid closed, until it releases easily from the grates, about 4 minutes. Turn and grill the other side until opaque all the way through, about 4 minutes. Set aside to cool for at least 10 minutes. Serve, with more pesto alongside if you like.

California Healthy Veggie Burgers

1 (15-ounce) can chickpeas, drained

2 tablespoons olive oil or avocado oil, plus more if needed

½ medium yellow onion, finely chopped

½ pound cremini and/or shiitake mushrooms, finely chopped

1½ cups freshly cooked short-grain brown rice, warm

½ cup fresh breadcrumbs

¼ cup finely shredded carrots

1 tablespoon tamari or soy sauce

½ teaspoon ground cumin

½ teaspoon smoked paprika

Fine sea salt and freshly ground black pepper

6 burger buns, split and toasted

6 large slices Cheddar or other melting cheese (optional)

Your favorite burger condiments

Sliced ripe tomato, pickles, pickled onions, and lettuce leaves, for topping (optional)

We promise you these homemade veggie burgers are so much better than the store-bought options. A mixture of chickpeas, brown rice, and mushrooms creates the foundation and plenty of spices and tamari amp up the flavor. The patties are best pan-fried, not grilled, which gives them a nice crispy crust. This isn't the recipe for leftover rice, so make sure you cook the rice just before forming the burgers as it helps bind them together.

In a large mixing bowl, using a potato masher or a fork, roughly mash the chickpeas to a coarse puree. Set aside.

In a large skillet over medium heat, warm 1 tablespoon of oil. Add the onions and cook, stirring, until starting to brown, about 4 minutes. Add the mushrooms and cook, stirring, until browned and their liquid evaporates, about 4 minutes. Transfer to the mixing bowl.

Add the warm rice, breadcrumbs, carrots, tamari, cumin, paprika, 1 teaspoon of salt, and ½ teaspoon of pepper to the mixing bowl. Stir to combine.

Divide the mixture into 6 equal portions (each about ½ cup) and press firmly into ½-inch-thick patties, each about 3½ inches in diameter. Place on a parchment paper–lined baking sheet.

Continues on page 101.

To cook: In the large skillet over medium-high heat, warm the remaining 1 tablespoon of oil. Add the patties in an even layer. Cook, turning once, until nicely browned on both sides, about 7 minutes. Add the cheese (if using) during the last 2 or 3 minutes of cooking. (Add more oil, if needed, to keep them from sticking.)

Spread the buns with the condiments of your choice, then layer the patty and toppings on the bottom bun. Cap with the top bun and serve at once.

Better-Than-a-Snack
Veggie Frito Pie

Not a lunch hour goes by at Bronson Alcott High without countless bags of assorted big-brand potato and corn chips littering the lunchroom tables. This hearty retro recipe is just the thing to get you through another boring school day or workday. You can make these directly in the bag, which is traditional, or add about 1½ cups of the corn chips to a bowl, then ladle the veggie chili over the top. This makes a bit more chili than you need for only 4 servings, but it freezes well and is great over baked potatoes, rice, or with cornbread.

VEGGIE CHILI
(MAKES 6 TO 7 CUPS)

2 tablespoons olive oil or avocado oil

½ yellow onion, finely chopped

1 small red bell pepper, seeded and finely chopped

½ small green bell pepper, seeded and finely chopped

1 small jalapeño pepper, seeded if desired, minced (optional)

Fine sea salt

3 tablespoons chili powder

1 (15-ounce) can red kidney beans, drained and rinsed

1 (15-ounce) can pinto beans, drained and rinsed

1 (15-ounce) can black beans, drained and rinsed

1 (14.5-ounce) can fire-roasted diced tomatoes with juices

1 (14.5-ounce) can tomato puree

1 cup water

Four 2-ounce bags of corn chips, preferably Fritos

2 ounces shredded Cheddar or Monterey Jack cheese

⅓ cup sliced black olives (optional)

½ cup sour cream (optional)

To make the chili: In a large saucepan over medium heat, warm the oil. Add the onions, bell peppers, and jalapeño pepper (if using) with a big pinch of salt and cook, stirring occasionally, until tender and starting to brown, about 8 minutes. Stir in the chili powder. Add the beans, diced tomatoes, tomato puree, and water. Bring to a boil, reduce the heat to low, and simmer, partially covered, until thick and fragrant, about 45 minutes. (The chili can be cooled to room temperature and stored in airtight containers in the refrigerator for up to 1 week, or frozen for up to 1 month. Re-warm before serving.)

To assemble: For each "pie," cut open a bag of the chips along one long edge. Ladle about ½ cup warm chili into the bag, then top with cheese, black olives, and sour cream, if using, and serve at once. Repeat with all the bags of chips. Alternatively, serve in bowls.

Extra Credit Steak Caesar Avocado Wraps

CAESAR DRESSING (MAKES 1 CUP)

1 large egg yolk

2 tablespoons freshly squeezed lemon juice

1 teaspoon Worcestershire sauce

½ teaspoon anchovy paste

1 clove garlic, minced

¼ cup (loosely packed) grated Parmesan cheese

⅓ cup avocado oil

¼ cup extra-virgin olive oil

Kosher salt and freshly ground black pepper

STEAK WRAPS

One 1-pound flank steak

Kosher salt and freshly ground black pepper

Extra-virgin olive oil, for drizzling

Four 10-inch flour or spinach tortillas

1 ripe but firm avocado, peeled, pitted, and thinly sliced

4 cups shredded romaine lettuce

¼ cup (loosely packed) grated Parmesan cheese

While serving her dad tea and cookies, Cher impresses him with her "upgraded" report card by arguing her way from a C+ to an A–. "Totally based on my powers of persuasion. You proud?" asks Cher. "Honey, I couldn't be happier than if they were based on real grades," he exclaims. Here we combine two favorite foods from the '90s—wraps and Caesar salads—and add some creamy California avocado slices and grilled steak for a definite upgrade, one you're sure to get extra credit for.

To make the dressing: In a measuring cup that just fits an immersion blender (or in a blender), combine the egg yolk, lemon juice, Worcestershire sauce, anchovy paste, garlic, and Parmesan. Blend together. With the blender running, slowly drizzle in the avocado oil until the mixture emulsifies. With the blender still running, slowly add the olive oil. Season with salt (if needed) and plenty of pepper. If the dressing is overly thick, thin it with a little water, 1 teaspoon at a time. Use at once or refrigerate until ready to use. The dressing can be stored in an airtight container in the refrigerator for up to 5 days.

To make the steak: Season the steak generously with salt and pepper, drizzle with olive oil, then rub about 2 tablespoons of the Caesar dressing all over the steak. Set aside at room temperature while you preheat the grill.

Continues on page 106.

Preheat a gas or charcoal grill for direct grilling over medium-high heat (about 450°F). Brush the grill grates clean. Grill the steak, with the lid closed, until it releases easily from the grates, about 5 minutes. Turn and grill the other side, until the steak is cooked to your liking, about 3 minutes longer for medium-rare (depending on the thickness of the steak). Transfer the steak to a cutting board, cover loosely with aluminum foil, and let it rest for 10 minutes. Thinly slice the steak against the grain; if you like, cut the slices crosswise into chunks.

To assemble the wraps: Lay out the tortillas on a clean work surface. Spread about 1 tablespoon of the dressing at the center of each tortilla. Arrange one-fourth of the avocado slices along the center of each tortilla on top of the dressing, leaving about a 1-inch border on the ends and space above and below. In a bowl, toss the lettuce and Parmesan with about ¼ cup dressing, then divide between the tortillas, arranging the salad on top of the avocado and leaving a border on the ends. Top the salad with steak, dividing it evenly between the tortillas. Roll up the tortilla like a burrito by folding the bottom of the tortilla up and over the filling, tucking in the sides, and rolling up tightly.

Cut each wrap in half on the diagonal and serve right away, or wrap each one in aluminum foil and take it to school to make all your friends jealous.

"TOTALLY BASED ON MY POWERS OF PERSUASION"

CHAPTER FIVE
Ditch-the-Diet Desserts

While most sweets don't figure into Cher's diet, they do make their way onto the lunchtime table, alongside tea in the afternoon, and as part of a celebration—say, at a wedding between two teachers after a successful fix-up (Vanilla "Wedding" Cupcakes, page 118). Apple Cookie Bar "Newtons" (page 112) and Devilish Marshmallow Cookie Cakes (page 124) are both based on popular '90s national brand cookies that make regular appearances throughout *Clueless*. The Math Teacher Candy Bar Cheesecake (page 121) is a tribute to Cher swooning over a Snickers bar being eaten by "the evil trolls from the math department [who] were actually married." And if you are ever trying to seduce someone, Desirable Chocolate Truffles (page 128) and Don't Burn the Chocolate Chip Cookies (page 130) should be top of the list.

DOUGH

½ cup unsalted butter, at room temperature

⅓ cup firmly packed light brown sugar

1½ tablespoons runny honey

½ teaspoon baking soda

¼ teaspoon ground cinnamon

¼ teaspoon fine sea salt

3 large egg yolks

2 tablespoons orange juice

8 ounces (about 2 cups) all-purpose flour

APPLE-FIG FILLING

1 large tart-sweet baking apple, such as Granny Smith, Honeycrisp, or Pink Lady

1 tablespoon unsalted butter

¼ cup firmly packed light brown sugar

3 ounces chopped dried Mission figs (½ cup packed)

1 cup boiling water

¼ cup pitted and chopped medjool dates (about 3 large dates)

¼ teaspoon ground cinnamon

¼ teaspoon fine sea salt

Apple Cookie Bar "Newtons"

Apple Newtons made their debut in 1986 and quickly became one of the more popular "healthy" cookies of the '90s—and a part of the lunchtime array at Cher's table, at least the fat-free versions. Eat them, share with friends, pack them for lunch, or use them to garnish your Beverly Hills Yogurt Parfaits (page 4) if you want to be extra fancy. Be sure to select plump and sticky dried figs so they help bind the filling together better.

To make the dough: In a medium mixing bowl, using an electric mixer, beat together the butter, sugar, honey, baking soda, cinnamon, and sea salt until creamy and well combined. Add the egg yolks and orange juice, and beat until well incorporated. Add the flour and beat on low speed just until combined. Form the dough into a disk, wrap tightly, and refrigerate for 30 minutes. (The dough can be refrigerated for up to 3 days; bring to cool room temperature before rolling.)

While the dough chills, make the filling. Peel and core the apple, then cut into small pieces. In a medium skillet over medium-low heat, melt the butter. Add the apple and cook, stirring, until tender, about 10 minutes. Stir in the brown sugar until well combined. Set aside to cool slightly.

Continues on page 114.

While the apples cook and cool, put the figs into a small heatproof bowl and add the boiling water. Let them sit for 15 minutes. Drain well in a fine-mesh sieve. Place the figs in the bowl of a food processor and pulse until very finely chopped. Add the apple mixture, dates, cinnamon, and salt to the figs, and process to a coarse puree. Scrape the filling into a piping bag fitted with a large round tip (½ inch); alternatively, transfer the filling to a zippered plastic bag and cut off one corner. Set aside.

Line a large, rimmed baking sheet with parchment paper.

On a lightly floured surface, roll out the dough into a rectangle that is about 11 by 14 inches and ¼-inch thick. Cut the dough crosswise into 4 strips, each 3½ inches wide. Pipe a 1-inch-thick log of filling down the middle of each strip. Fold one long edge over the filling, brushing off any excess flour, then roll the log over onto the other edge so the dough is seam side down. Carefully transfer the log to the baking sheet and gently flatten. Refrigerate for 15 minutes.

While the bars chill, preheat the oven to 350°F.

Bake until firm and lightly puffed, about 15 minutes. Remove from the oven and immediately cut the bars crosswise into 1-inch pieces. Cover the bars with a piece of parchment paper and let cool on the baking sheet on a wire rack. When cooled to room temperature, cover the baking sheet with plastic wrap and set aside for about 3 hours so the cookies soften. Serve.

PIE DOUGH

2½ cups all-purpose flour

½ teaspoon fine sea salt

1 tablespoon sugar

1 cup (8 ounces) very cold unsalted butter, diced

11 tablespoons ice water, plus more if needed

PIE FILLING

¾ cup granulated sugar, or more or less depending on the sweetness of the fruit

¼ cup tapioca starch, depending on the juiciness of the fruit

8 ripe peaches (peeled) or nectarines, pitted and sliced (about 6 heaping cups)

Juice of ½ lemon

1 large egg, beaten with 1 teaspoon water, for egg wash

Tai Lattice Peach Pie

When Tai first arrives at Bronson Alcott High School, she sits down at Cher's table with a slice of pie and a carton of milk, while Cher offers her sage advice—she is, after all, one month older than Tai—about who Tai should and shouldn't spend time with at school if she wants to be popular. Lunchtime pie is a treat, especially if it's a homemade peach pie and not one from the lunch line at the school cafeteria. Making this will almost guarantee your popularity.

Note: You can use this technique for virtually any summer fruit; just use 6 heaping cups pitted and sliced stone fruits and/or berries and increase or decrease the amount of sugar and thickener depending on the sweetness and juiciness of the fruit.

To make the pie dough: In the bowl of a food processor, pulse together the flour, salt, and sugar. Sprinkle the butter over the top and pulse until the butter is about the size of peas. Evenly sprinkle the water over the flour mixture, then process just until the mixture starts to come together. Dump the dough onto a work surface, press it together, then divide it in half. Press each half into a disk, then wrap the disks with plastic wrap. Refrigerate for 30 minutes or up to 1 day, or freeze for up to 1 month.

Continues on page 117.

Roll out each dough disk into a round about 12 inches in diameter and about ⅛-inch thick. Line a 9-inch pie pan with 1 round, trimming the dough as needed to leave a 1-inch overhang. Place the lined pie dish and second dough round into the refrigerator to chill while you prepare the filling.

To make the filling: In a large bowl, stir together the sugar and tapioca starch. Add the peaches or nectarines and lemon juice and toss to combine. Let stand while you cut the dough strips for the lattice top.

Position a rack in the lower third of the oven and preheat the oven to 400°F. Remove the pie pan and dough round from the refrigerator. Using a 1-inch-wide ruler as a guide, cut the dough round into 9 or 10 even strips.

Spoon the fruit mixture, including the juices, into the chilled pastry shell in an even layer. Lay 5 strips of dough evenly across the top, using the longest strips in the center and the shorter strips on the sides. Fold back every other strip halfway and lay down a strip perpendicular across the unfolded strips. Repeat to place 4 or 5 strips of dough evenly across the top, folding back the alternate strips each time. Trim the ends of the strips so they are even with the bottom crust. Tuck the dough under itself to create a rim. Use your fingers or a fork to flute the rim. Place the prepared pie on a baking sheet.

Brush the top of the crust all over with the egg wash.

Bake for 30 minutes, then reduce the oven temperature to 375°F and continue to bake until the crust is deep golden brown and the fruit juices are thickened and bubbling, about 30 to 40 minutes longer. If the crust starts to get too brown, lay a piece of foil over the top. Let the pie cool completely before slicing, at least 4 hours (this helps it set).

VANILLA CUPCAKES

1¾ cups cake flour

1 cup granulated sugar

2 teaspoons baking powder

½ teaspoon baking soda

½ teaspoon fine sea salt

5 tablespoons unsalted butter, at room temperature, cut into chunks

2 large eggs

½ cup sour cream (not low fat)

½ cup whole milk

¼ cup avocado or canola oil

1 tablespoon pure vanilla extract

VANILLA FROSTING

1 cup unsalted butter, at room temperature

5 cups confectioners' sugar, sifted

6 tablespoons whole milk

1 tablespoon pure vanilla extract

Pinch of fine sea salt

Sparkle sugar or other sprinkles, for decorating

Vanilla "Wedding" Cupcakes

Spoiler alert: Mr. Hall and Miss Geist get married! And what wedding would be complete without a big, white vanilla cake (especially in the '90s)? Relive that special wedding moment with these dazzling double vanilla cupcakes, decorated with sparkle sugar. At the Hall-Geist wedding, Tai and Dionne start talking about what they would wear to their own weddings while Travis, Murray, and Josh look on, and Josh eats a huge piece of wedding cake. Murray exclaims (in true Murray fashion), "OMG, they're planning our weddings already!"

To make the cupcakes: Preheat the oven to 350°F. Line about 20 cups of two standard muffin pans with paper or foil liners, or spray well with cooking spray.

Sift the flour, sugar, baking powder, baking soda, and salt into the bowl of a stand mixer. Add the butter and mix on medium-low speed until the mixture looks like breadcrumbs, about 1 minute.

In another bowl, whisk together the eggs, sour cream, milk, oil, and vanilla. Add the egg mixture to the flour mixture and beat on medium speed just until combined. The batter will be very thin.

Scoop up the batter and divide it between the muffin cups, filling them no more than ⅔ full (a ¼-cup measure works well for this).

Continues on page 120.

Bake until puffed and a toothpick inserted into the center of a cupcake comes out with only moist crumbs attached, about 15 minutes (they will be only very lightly golden). Let cool for 5 minutes in the pan, then remove the cupcakes and set on a wire rack to cool completely.

To make the frosting: In the bowl of a stand mixer, beat the butter on medium speed until light and creamy. Add the confectioners' sugar, milk, vanilla, and salt. Mix on low speed just until combined. Scrape down the bowl with a rubber spatula. Beat on medium-high speed until the frosting is fluffy and smooth. Transfer the frosting to a piping bag fitted with a medium or large star tip.

Pipe the frosting onto the cupcakes, dividing it evenly. Sprinkle with the sparkle sugar for some extra va-va-voom. Celebrate!

MAKES
ONE
9-INCH
CHEESECAKE;
SERVES
10 TO 12

CHOCOLATE-PEANUT CRUST

4 ounces chocolate graham crackers or 5½ ounces crisp chocolate wafer cookies

⅓ cup roasted unsalted peanuts

4 tablespoons unsalted butter, melted, plus more for greasing the pan

2 tablespoons sugar

Pinch of fine sea salt

CHOCOLATE-VANILLA SWIRL FILLING

4 ounces bittersweet chocolate, chopped

2 tablespoons whole milk

3 (8-ounce) packages cream cheese, at room temperature

1 cup granulated sugar

½ cup sour cream

2 teaspoons vanilla extract

4 large eggs

2 tablespoons all-purpose flour

TOPPING

About ½ cup thick caramel sauce

¼ cup roasted unsalted peanuts

About 1 cup chopped candy bars, preferably Snickers

Whipped Cream (page 150)

Math Teacher Candy Bar Cheesecake

"The evil trolls from the math department" who were "actually married" share a Snickers candy bar for their lunch in the teachers' lounge while Cher homes in on the candy: "Oooohhh, Snickers." Make all your candy bar dreams come true with this Snickers-inspired cheesecake. A crunchy chocolate wafer–peanut crust, chocolate-vanilla swirled cheesecake, and toppings galore—think gooey caramel sauce, chunks of candy bar, and clouds of whipped cream—are enough to make you swoon.

Preheat the oven to 325°F. Lightly grease a 9-inch springform pan with butter, then line the bottom with parchment paper. Butter the top of the parchment. Wrap a double-thick layer of aluminum foil around the outside of the pan to better insulate it.

To make the crust: In the bowl of a food processor, combine the graham crackers or wafer cookies and peanuts. Process until finely ground. Add the butter, sugar, and salt and pulse until the crumbs are evenly moistened and stick together when pressed. Press the crumbs evenly into the bottom and 1 inch up the side of the prepared pan. Bake until set, about 10 minutes. Set aside on a wire rack while you make the filling.

Continues on page 123.

To make the filling: Melt the chocolate and milk in the microwave or a small saucepan, then set aside to cool to room temperature. In the clean bowl of a food processor, process the cream cheese and sugar on medium speed until smooth, about 2 minutes. Scrape down the sides of the bowl with a rubber spatula. Add the sour cream and vanilla and process until blended. Add the eggs one at a time, processing after each addition. Add the flour and process until combined. Scrape down the bowl, and process once more.

Pour half of the batter into a bowl. This will be the vanilla batter. Add the cooled chocolate mixture to the remaining batter in the food processor and process until smooth and well combined. Pour half of the vanilla filling into the prepared springform pan, then pour half of the chocolate filling over the vanilla. Add the remaining vanilla filling, and then the remaining chocolate filling. Use a small spatula or paring knife to gently swirl the fillings around and create a marbled effect.

Bake until the cheesecake is set but still a little jiggly in the center, about 50 minutes. Turn off the oven, prop open the oven door, and leave the cheesecake for 1 hour. Remove from the oven. Let the cheesecake cool completely on a wire rack.

Cover the pan with plastic wrap (not touching the surface of the cheesecake) and refrigerate until chilled, at least 3 hours or overnight.

To serve: Cut into wedges. Top each wedge with a drizzle of caramel sauce, roasted peanuts, chopped candy bars, and a dollop of whipped cream (or pipe it on, using a star tip for a neater appearance). Drizzle with more caramel sauce if you like, and then completely destroy your diet (happily!).

½ cup unsalted butter, at room temperature

½ cup firmly packed light brown sugar

1 large egg

1 teaspoon vanilla extract

¼ teaspoon fine sea salt

¾ cup all-purpose flour

½ cup natural cocoa powder

½ teaspoon baking powder

½ teaspoon baking soda

¾ cup marshmallow crème

8 ounces semisweet chocolate chips

3 tablespoons avocado or canola oil

Devilish Marshmallow Cookie Cakes

When Tai has a "brush with death at the mall," the entire high school is fascinated, and everyone surrounds Tai at lunch, wanting to hear more. Front and center on the lunch table is a pile of devil's food cookie cakes (fat-free, of course). "Right before you die, your mind just sort of gets very clear," says Tai, as Cher looks on, dumbstruck, and can't get a word in edgewise. She's none too thrilled that Tai is getting all the attention, and she's getting nothing— nothing a pile of devil's food chocolate cookies topped with marshmallow and covered with thin melted chocolate can't help, though!

Position 2 oven racks evenly in the oven and preheat to 350°F. Line 2 baking sheets with parchment paper.

In a bowl, using an electric mixer, beat together the butter and brown sugar on medium-high speed until creamy. Add the egg, vanilla, and salt, and beat until well combined. Sift the flour, cocoa, baking powder, and baking soda into the bowl and mix on low speed just until combined.

Using a small cookie scoop, scoop up a heaping table-spoonful of the dough. Arrange the dough balls on the prepared baking sheets, dividing them evenly. You should have 12 to 13 dough balls.

Continues on page 126.

Bake until puffed and slightly firm, about 8 minutes, rotating the pans between racks halfway through baking. As soon as the cookies come out of the oven, slam the baking sheet down on a hard surface to flatten them slightly (alternatively, use a metal spatula to flatten them slightly). Set aside the pans to cool for 5 minutes, then use a metal spatula to transfer the cookies to a wire rack to cool completely.

When the cookies are cool, spread the top of each with 1 tablespoon of marshmallow crème. Transfer to a small baking sheet or tray and freeze for 15 minutes.

In a heatproof bowl set over barely simmering water, melt the chocolate chips and oil. Alternatively, melt the chocolate and oil together in a microwave-safe bowl, stirring about every 20 seconds, until melted. Let cool slightly.

Transfer the cookies to a rack set over a piece of parchment. Line a small baking sheet or tray with parchment paper. Using a soup spoon, spoon the chocolate mixture over the tops of the cookies in an even layer to cover the top and sides. Let sit for a few minutes for the glaze to drip off, then carefully transfer the cookies to the parchment-lined baking sheet. Freeze until the chocolate is set, about 15 to 30 minutes. Serve.

The cookies can be stored in an airtight container, separated by parchment paper, in the refrigerator for up to 1 week.

"TOTALLY BUGGIN'"

1 cup heavy whipping cream

9 ounces bittersweet or semisweet chocolate, chopped

½ teaspoon finely grated orange zest or vanilla extract, or ¼ teaspoon peppermint extract (optional)

Unsweetened cocoa powder, chocolate sprinkles, or finely chopped toasted nuts

Desirable Chocolate Truffles

After Cher meets Christian, she decides to make sure he knows how "desirable" she is by sending herself flowers, love letters, and chocolates in class. Homemade truffles are a snap to make, with only a handful of ingredients. And you can personalize them with whatever you like— orange zest, vanilla, or mint. Go ahead and send yourself some flowers, too. You deserve it!

In a saucepan over medium-low heat, warm the cream just until steaming. Remove from the heat and add the chocolate, along with the orange zest or extract, if using. Set aside for 2 minutes to give the chocolate a chance to melt in the warm cream. Stir gently with a whisk until the chocolate is melted and the mixture is well combined. Scrape into a bowl and press a piece of plastic wrap directly onto the surface of the mixture. Refrigerate until the mixture is solid, at least 2 hours or overnight.

Line a baking sheet with parchment paper. Using a small cookie scoop or a melon baller, scoop out about 1 tablespoon of the chocolate mixture, then quickly roll it into a ball. Repeat, arranging the truffles on the prepared baking sheet. If the truffles soften or start to melt, return them to the refrigerator to firm up before proceeding.

Roll the truffles in cocoa powder, sprinkles, or nuts. Serve right away or refrigerate for up to 4 days in an airtight container with parchment paper between the layers.

½ cup unsalted butter, at room temperature

⅔ cup firmly packed light brown sugar

⅔ cup granulated sugar

½ teaspoon fine sea salt

1 large egg

1 large egg yolk

2 teaspoons vanilla extract

2 cups all-purpose flour

1 teaspoon baking soda

½ teaspoon baking powder

2 cups mixed chocolate chips, such as bittersweet, semisweet, milk, and/or white

Don't Burn the Chocolate Chip Cookies

"Whenever a boy comes, you should always have something baking," Cher explains as she heaves an entire roll of premade chocolate chip cookie dough onto a baking sheet and puts it in the oven. Of course, Cher gets distracted and forgets about it and burns the log of dough. Make sure to set a timer when baking these crispy-chewy chocolate chip cookies—they are so good that you definitely don't want to burn them. Plus, they smell a lot nicer when smoke isn't billowing out of the oven.

Position 2 oven racks evenly in the oven and preheat to 375°F. Line 2 large, rimmed baking sheets with parchment paper.

In the bowl of a stand mixer, beat the butter, sugars, and salt on medium speed until light and creamy. Add the whole egg, the egg yolk, and vanilla, and beat until well combined. Scrape down the sides of the bowl. Add the flour, baking soda, and baking powder, and beat on low speed just until blended. Add the chocolate chips and beat just until combined.

Scoop up 2 ounces of dough, roll into a loose ball, and arrange 8 or 9 dough balls on each baking sheet, spacing them 2 inches apart. Press the dough lightly into 1-inch-thick disks. (The dough balls can be arranged on a small baking sheet, covered, and frozen for up to 3 months.)

Bake until light golden brown, rotating the pans halfway through, about 10 to 13 minutes. As soon as the cookies come out of the oven, use a spatula to gently flatten the cookies slightly.

Let cool on the pan for 5 minutes, then transfer the cookies to a wire rack to cool completely. Store in an airtight container at room temperature for up to 5 days.

LEMON SUGAR COOKIES

1 large egg

1 tablespoon lemon juice

1 teaspoon vanilla extract

¼ teaspoon lemon extract

2 cups all-purpose flour

1 cup granulated sugar

1 tablespoon packed finely grated lemon zest

½ teaspoon fine sea salt

½ teaspoon baking soda

¼ teaspoon baking powder

½ cup unsalted butter, at room temperature, cut into chunks

ROYAL ICING

2 ounces pasteurized egg whites, at room temperature

¼ teaspoon cream of tartar

Pinch of salt

2⅔ cups confectioners' sugar, sifted (or as needed)

Yellow and blue gel food coloring

Cute Plaid Lemon Sugar Cookies

There is almost nothing more iconic from *Clueless* than Cher's yellow, blue, and white plaid outfit, which she picks out at the start of the movie using a computer program in her closet. Her best friend, Dionne, wears a matching black, white, and red version of Cher's blazer and skirt. Dionne is Cher's friend "because we both know what it's like to have people be jealous of us . . . I must give her snaps for her courageous fashion efforts." These totally cute blue-and-yellow lemon sugar cookies will get full snaps for being adorable *and* yummy.

To make the cookies: In a small bowl, whisk together the egg, lemon juice, and vanilla and lemon extracts. In a mixing bowl, using a stand mixer with the paddle attachment, stir together the flour, sugar, lemon zest, salt, baking soda, and baking powder on low speed. Add the butter and mix on low speed until the butter breaks up into small pieces and the mixture looks like breadcrumbs, about 2 minutes. Add the egg mixture and beat on medium-low speed until the dough comes together. Press the dough into a disk, wrap in plastic wrap, and refrigerate for 30 minutes or overnight.

Continues on page 134.

Line a baking sheet with parchment paper. On a lightly floured work surface, roll out the dough into a round about ¼ inch thick. Using a 3½-inch round or fluted cookie cutter (or any shape you like!), cut out rounds, then transfer to the prepared baking sheet, spacing the cookies about 1 inch apart. Press the dough scraps together, re-roll, and cut out more rounds. When the baking sheet is full, lay another piece of parchment over the top of the dough rounds and fill with more dough rounds. Continue until all the dough is rolled and cut. Refrigerate for 15 minutes.

Position 2 oven racks evenly in the oven and preheat the oven to 350°F. Transfer one layer of cookies to another baking sheet, leaving the first layer on the first baking sheet (if you have additional layers, refrigerate those until you're ready to bake).

Bake the cookies, rotating the pans between racks halfway through, until golden, about 10 to 12 minutes total. Let cool on the pans on a wire rack for 15 minutes, then transfer the cookies to the rack. Repeat to bake the rest of the cookies, if needed.

To make the icing: In a bowl, using a stand mixer with the whisk attachment, beat the egg whites, cream of tartar, and salt on medium-low speed until blended. With the machine running, slowly add the sugar. Increase the speed to medium-high and beat until thick, stiff, and glossy, about 5 minutes. If the icing is too thick, thin it with a few drops of water until it is a smooth, pipable consistency.

Put about two-thirds of the icing into one bowl, then divide the remaining icing between two other bowls. Add drops of yellow food coloring to the first bowl, then add blue food coloring to the second bowl, and leave the third bowl white (you should mostly have yellow icing). Stir each to combine, adding more food coloring to get your desired color.

To decorate the cookies, transfer the blue, white, and about a quarter of the yellow icing into 3 different piping bags fitted with small round tips. Use the yellow icing to pipe an outline around each cookie; let set for 15 minutes. Thin the remaining yellow icing in the bowl and use it to "flood" the cookies within the outline. Let set for at least 1 hour or overnight.

Pipe a grid pattern with the blue and white icings. Let set until completely dry. Serve.

Full-on Monet Raspberry Vanilla Fro-Yo

12 ounces fresh raspberries (about 2 cups), plus more for serving

⅔ cup granulated sugar, divided

¼ cup raspberry jam

1 tablespoon freshly squeezed lemon juice

1½ cups plain whole-milk yogurt

½ cup heavy whipping cream

½ teaspoon vanilla extract

Fresh mint sprigs, for serving (optional)

Fro-yo became trendy in the late '80s and early '90s and was often seen as a healthy dessert alternative. Not surprisingly, the gossipy lunch hour with Cher and her friends often showcases cartons of fruit-flavored (low-fat, of course) yogurt and cans of Diet Coke. Gossip doesn't only happen around the lunch table, though. At the school dance, Tai looks at Amber and asks Cher if she thinks Amber is pretty. Cher replies, "No, she's a full-on Monet!" Tai questions, "What's a Monet?" And Cher gives her an art history lesson: "It's like a painting, see? From far away, it's okay, but up close it's a big old mess." This pretty pink fro-yo is no mess, though. It's easy to make and certain to make quite an impression.

Note: Be sure to chill the raspberry puree and the yogurt mixture well before freezing the mixture in your ice cream maker. You can use other berries for this as well; just use equal amounts of sliced strawberries or blackberries instead of raspberries.

In a saucepan over medium heat, combine the raspberries, ⅓ cup of the sugar, the jam, and the lemon juice. Using a potato masher or a large fork, mash and stir the raspberries to make a thick paste. Bring to a gentle boil, then cook, stirring, until the juices thicken, about 8 minutes.

Continues on page 138.

Transfer to a fine-mesh sieve set over a bowl. Using a rubber spatula, press the raspberry mixture through the sieve. Discard the seeds. You should have about 1¼ cups. Cover the bowl of raspberry puree and refrigerate until very cold, at least 1 hour.

Add the remaining ⅓ cup sugar, yogurt, cream, and vanilla to the raspberry puree. Refrigerate until the mixture is very cold, at least 2 hours or overnight. Freeze in an ice cream machine, according to the manufacturer's instructions. Enjoy right away or transfer to a freezer-safe, airtight container, cover, and freeze until firm.

Serve scoops with some fresh raspberries and mint sprigs to make it extra pretty!

DIONNE:

Uh, no, Ms. Stoeger? I have a note from my tennis instructor, and he would prefer it if I didn't expose myself to any training that might derail his teachings.

MS. STOEGER:

Fine! Amber?

AMBER:

Ms. Stoeger, my plastic surgeon doesn't want me doing any activity where balls fly at my nose.

DIONNE:

Well, there goes your social life.

CHAPTER SIX

Makeover Drinks

The diet soda is flowing in nearly every scene in *Clueless*, but a girl can't live on diet drinks alone—unless of course it's a Dirty Diet Coke Mocktail (page 152). If you and your friends are hanging out at the mall soda fountain, flirting, you'll want to order up some Not-the-Mall-Food-Court Smoothies (page 146) and Soda Fountain Chocolate Milkshakes (page 150). Totally Decadent Mochaccinos (page 154) might ease the sting of failing your driver's test and getting in a fight with your bestie, but we promise they won't make you feel like a "ralphing heifer."

MAKES 2 LARGE OR 4 SMALL SMOOTHIES

1 cup fresh mango chunks, frozen

1 cup chopped fresh pineapple, frozen

1 cup chopped frozen strawberries

1 cup orange juice

Agave syrup or honey, to taste

2 tablespoons plain or vanilla protein powder (optional)

Dad's Healthy Tropical "Vitamin C" Orange Smoothies

In an effort to keep her dad healthy ("Daddy, you need your vitamin C"), Cher makes him freshly squeezed orange juice in the mornings—which he refuses to drink. "He gets $500 an hour to fight with people, but he fights with me for free because I'm his daughter," she explains. Orange juice, mango, pineapple, and strawberries are all high in vitamin C, giving this tropical smoothie a quadruple whammy of healthfulness.

Place the mango, pineapple, strawberries, orange juice, ¼ cup water, 1 teaspoon agave syrup, and protein powder (if using) in a high-speed blender and blend until smooth. Add a little more water if the smoothie is too thick. Sweeten to taste with additional agave syrup if you like. Divide between glasses and serve.

1 cup fresh orange juice (not from concentrate)

½ ripe avocado, pitted, peeled, and cubed

½ cup packed baby spinach

½ cup vanilla yogurt

¼ cup milk of choice

2 teaspoons agave syrup or honey, or to taste

½ teaspoon vanilla extract

2 (1-ounce) wheatgrass juice shots (optional)

Not-the-Mall-Food-Court Smoothies

This dreamy I-can't-believe-it's-not-ice-cream orange and vanilla smoothie is reminiscent of the mall-time favorite "Orange Julius," but made with healthier ingredients and no processed sugar. As if! The sneaky addition of spinach and avocado might seem odd, but they really work. For extra California healthiness, pair these smoothies with ultra-healthy wheatgrass shots (but make sure to sip the smoothie afterward to get rid of that '90s taste).

Place the orange juice in an ice cube tray and freeze until solid. Place the avocado, spinach, yogurt, milk, agave, and vanilla in a high-speed blender and blend until smooth. Divide the smoothie between 2 glasses. Take a wheatgrass juice shot and then chase it with the smoothie.

4 scoops vanilla ice cream

1 (12-ounce) bottle root beer

Whipped Cream (page 150)

3 tablespoons store-bought
  caramel sauce

Root Beer "Pool Party" Floats

At the ragin' party in the Valley, Murray gets his head shaved, a game of "suck and blow" raises eyebrows, there's singing and dancing and fashion put-downs, and a whole lot of kids end up jumping into the pool. These pool party "floats" might just make your next "rager" full of wild, festive fun. They are super easy to throw together: Just choose your favorite root beer and your favorite vanilla ice cream. One 12-ounce bottle of root beer makes 2 large servings, or you can make 4 mini floats in smaller glasses with 1 scoop of ice cream each and the root beer divided among the 4 glasses.

For each float, place 2 scoops of ice cream in a pint glass. Pour half the root beer into the glass. Top with a big dollop of whipped cream, then drizzle with half the caramel sauce. Repeat for the second serving. Serve at once.

WHIPPED CREAM (MAKES ABOUT 1 CUP)

½ cup heavy whipping cream

1 tablespoon granulated sugar

½ teaspoon vanilla extract

CHOCOLATE SHAKE

3 large scoops (about 8 ounces; 1½ cups) of your favorite vanilla ice cream

½ cup whole milk

3 to 4 tablespoons good-quality chocolate syrup, plus more for garnish

1 to 2 cherries (optional)

Soda Fountain Chocolate Milkshakes

The opening scene of *Clueless*, to the tune of "We're the Kids in America," helps set the tone for what's to come. Drinking whipped cream–topped chocolate milkshakes, Cher and her two best friends laugh and flirt at the soda fountain as Dionne feeds the guy working there a cherry. For an extra-chocolaty shake, use chocolate ice cream. Use any kind of cherry you like—maraschino, Amarena, or fresh bing cherries—just make sure it has a stem!

To make the whipped cream: In a small bowl, combine the cream, sugar, and vanilla. Using a handheld electric mixer or a whisk, beat the cream until soft to medium peaks form. Do not overwhip. Use right away or cover and refrigerate for up to 1 day; rewhip the cream if it loosens.

To make the milkshake: Place the ice cream, milk, and chocolate syrup in a blender. Cover and blend on medium-high speed, stopping once or twice to scrape down the sides if needed, until thick and creamy. Transfer to a tall fountain glass or divide between 2 glasses.

Top with a dollop of whipped cream, a drizzle of syrup, and a cherry on top (if using).

Dirty Diet Coke Mocktails

2 tablespoons freshly squeezed lime juice

1 tablespoon coconut syrup, or to taste

1 (12-ounce) can diet cola, preferably Diet Coke

2 tablespoons heavy whipping cream

2 lime wedges, for serving

Rarely do you see Cher at lunchtime without her can of Diet Coke. This mocktail doctors up the iconic diet soda with lime juice, coconut syrup, and cream, making it as unique as Cher's ability to make all the students love her when she gets Mr. Hall and Miss Geist together. "The entire student body was utterly grateful for the improvement in their grades," smiles Cher as she twirls and curtsies to the applause of her fellow students, all while sipping Diet Coke. Take things up a notch and add a shot of rum to each mocktail, if you like!

In each of 2 rocks glasses, place 1 tablespoon lime juice and ½ tablespoon coconut syrup. Fill each glass with ice, then divide the diet cola between the 2 glasses. Use a barspoon to gently stir the mixture in each glass. Top each with 1 tablespoon of cream. Taste and add a little more coconut syrup if you like. Garnish each with a lime wedge and serve.

DIONNE:
Oh, my god. Look.
Is that a photo op or what?

CHER:
Will you look at that body
language? Legs crossed
toward each other. That's
an unequivocal sex invite.

DIONNE:
Oh, Cher, he's getting
her digits. Look at Geist,
she is so cute.

CHER:
Ohh, old people
can be so sweet.

Whipped Cream (page 150)

2 tablespoons (or to taste) chocolate syrup, plus more for garnish

2 cups hot, strong, freshly brewed coffee

Chocolate shavings or sprinkles

Totally Decadent Mochaccinos

After Tai confides in Cher that she likes Josh, Cher gets visibly upset. Cher explains that she "was really bad today, I had two mochaccinos. I feel like ralphing." Cher then tries to gently tell Tai she doesn't think that she and Josh "mesh well together." Tai gets angry and asks Cher why she's even listening to her to begin with since she's a virgin who can't drive! Ouch. "Oh, that was way harsh, Tai," says Cher.

Note: A mochaccino is a mash-up of a cappuccino and a mocha coffee, topped with foamy milk. This decadent version takes that over the top with a cloud of whipped cream and chocolate shavings. To make chocolate shavings, use a vegetable peeler to peel away shavings from a chunk of semisweet or bittersweet chocolate.

Make the whipped cream and transfer to a piping bag fitted with a star tip. (Alternatively, you can dollop the whipped cream on top with a spoon.) Set aside.

In each of 2 mugs, place 1 tablespoon of chocolate syrup (or add as much as you'd like!). Pour the hot coffee over the chocolate syrup, filling each mug about two-thirds to three-fourths full. Stir to combine the coffee and chocolate syrup.

Immediately top each coffee with the whipped cream (as much as you like), garnish with the chocolate shavings, and drizzle with a little more chocolate syrup. Serve at once.

Acknowledgments

As a child of the '80s and '90s, I found this book so much fun to write. Taking a deep dive into this nostalgic, classic movie was like returning to my teenage years and early adulthood. I have to thank my wonderful mom, Ann Crowder, and my dear (late) father, Al Crowder, for their patience and guidance through that tumultuous and formative time.

Fast-forward to the present, and my mom is still by my side, along with my husband, Keith Laidlaw, and our daughter, Poppy, who loves to bake, cook, and help me come up with ideas for recipes to put in my books. Thank you, Poppy, for being so creative and always inspirational, and willing to try just about anything I cook. And a huge thank-you to my amazing husband, who is my rock, my biggest cheerleader, and also does most of the dishes. An extra-special thank-you to my dear mum-in-law, Pauline Laidlaw, who, when visiting from Scotland, relishes every dessert I develop, while also helping with the never-ending dishes.

Thank you to my dear friends (and their kids!), aka my taste testers, always willing to give me feedback, cheer me on, and make sure I don't waste any food: Brittany Ceres, Hannah Eaves, Wendy Goodfriend, Natasha Hauswald (and her mom, Susan), Deanie Hickox, Ingrid Keir, and Noelle Moss. To my neighbors and my husband's coworking colleagues and friends who always accept my crazy platters of food and enjoy them with gusto (cake for breakfast!).

An enormous thank-you to my editor, Jordana Hawkins, who reached out to me to take on this entertaining project, book designer Jenna McBride, production editor Leah Gordon, publicist Annie Brag, marketer Amy Cianfrone, publisher Kristin Kiser, and everyone at Running Press. And to Risa Kessler and Sabi Lofgren at Paramount Global Consumer Products, who shared my name with my book editor and helped connect us. It's been truly great to have all your support. Thank you, thank you.

Index

About the Author

KIM LAIDLAW is a cookbook author, editor, and recipe developer. She is the author or coauthor of ten cookbooks, including bestsellers *The Nightmare Before Christmas Cookbook*, *Emily in Paris: The Official Cookbook*, *Five Marys Ranch Raised Cookbook*, and numerous Williams Sonoma cookbooks. Kim has managed hundreds of cookbook projects, including Kendall-Jackson's *SEASON*, winner of the 2019 IACP Book of the Year. Her clients include Disney, Netflix, Weber, Hog Island, KitchenAid, American Girl, and more. She is a former professional baker and baking instructor at the San Francisco Cooking School and owns Cast Iron Media, LLC. Kim lives in Petaluma, California, with her Scottish husband, their always-entertaining daughter, and a bountiful home garden.